Do You Need Psychic Protection?

Absolutely—and a dynamic, powerful, psychic aura is your best defense. A strong aura will shield you not only from the stresses, pressures, and "psychic noise" that surround you every day—it will also recharge and invigorate your life force, give your immune system a boost, and guard you from physical harm.

This book explains the basic principles and most effective methods of psychic self-defense so you can master them and adapt them to your own needs. Use psychic self-defense in your home, your workplace, even within your community, to create a haven from day-to-day worries, negative energy, and stress.

About the Authors

Melita Denning and Osborne Phillips are internationally recognized authorities on the mainstream Western Mysteries and the Ogdoadic Tradition, that premier hermetic school whose keywords are knowledge and regeneration.

The authors received their major esoteric training in the magical order Aurum Solis, a society that was founded in 1897 and that has continued in active existence to the present day. On July 8, 1987, the authors, then heads of Aurum Solis, retired from the order; but on June 23, 1988, at the unanimous request of the members, they resumed office.

Melita Denning passed over in 1996.

Practical Guide to

Psychic
Self-Defense

Strengthen Your Aura

DENNING & PHILLIPS

Llewellyn Publications
Woodbury, Minnesota

Third Edition
Twelfth Printing, 2016

Book design by Pam Keesey and Kimberly Nightingale
Cover design by William Merlin Cannon

Library of Congress Cataloging-in-Publication Data

Denning, Melita.
Practical guide to psychic self-defense & well-being. Reprint. Originally published: 2nd ed., rev. & enl. St. Paul, Minn.: Llewellyn Publications, 1983
  1. Occult sciences. I. Psychical research. 3. Self-defense—Miscellanea. I. Phillips, Osborne. II. Title. III. Title: Psychic self-defense & well-being. IV. Title: Psychic self-defense & well-being.
BF1999.D36
1986
131 83–80169
ISBN 13: 978-0-87542-190-2
ISBN 10: 0-87542-190-3

Llewellyn Worldwide does not participate in, endorse, or have any authority or responsibility concerning private business transactions between our authors and the public.
  All mail addressed to the author is forwarded but the publisher cannot, unless specifically instructed by the author, give out an address or phone number.
  Any Internet references contained in this work are current at publication time, but the publisher cannot guarantee that a specific location will continue to be maintained. Please refer to the publisher's website for links to authors' websites and other sources.

Llewellyn Publications
A Division of Llewellyn Worldwide Ltd.
2143 Wooddale Drive
Woodbury, MN 55125-2989
www.llewellyn.com
Llewellyn is a registered trademark of Llewellyn Worldwide Ltd.

Printed in the United States of America

We all have natural defenses within which we live and move, and we can use natural means to make these defenses stronger yet.

Contents

methods of fortifying the aura. Full confidence can be placed upon the aura's effectiveness in psychic defense, provided you do not open or weaken it from within. Using your fortified aura to defend yourself, your children, your home, your pets.

pire as a factor in alcoholism and in hypersexuality. Possibilities of human agency in such cases. Counter measures. Doll sorcery and counter measures. More on guardianship of the imagination.

5 Meeting Impersonal Aggression 123

Even where there is no ill-will involved, we can still suffer some danger from our environment. Stress, noise, some types of music, some types of drugs such as psychic self-defense painkillers, the conventional urgency of external tasks, all can weaken our self-awareness and lower our confidence. Necessity of taking time and action to revitalize ourselves. Desirability of a positive program, vacations spent in activities in which we feel we belong to our real selves. Importance of taking a few minutes in the course of the working day to "get back to source," and renew our spiritual contacts. The "inward glance." Diet and defense. Harmony within oneself, harmony with the natural world: essentials for psychic self-defense. People who can command rats and mice.

6 How to Survive in Business Life 145

Group mind and group aura: group aura and your aura in business life. "Office politics"and the individual. Keeping your nerves intact. Work well, play well. Why not do your own personality trip? Finding allies. The question of loyalty. Shopping for groceries, shopping for a house. Go on doing your own thinking. Psychological coercions and how to counter them: the three chief "push-buttons" and how they work. The word people fear even to utter; a vital morale practice for you, and a step toward a saner society.

Dealing with people who take favors for granted, rights-robbing bosses and relatives, sales callers, religious canvassers, professional gamblers, dead-loss lovers. How we take their side against ourselves: the irrational fear of "miss- ing a good thing." What the judge felt he had to say for the con man.

The interaction of life's levels, material and nonmaterial. Amulets: material focal points for nonmaterial influences. You can make or find your own. Preparing materials for use in amulets or in ritual. High value of ritual for psychic defense as a supplement to the development of the aura. Directions for ritual procedures: group ritual for protection of all participants, group ritual for the protection of one person, rapid emergency defense procedure for one person, the Rite of the First Kathisma for one person or many. The forward look: "luck"and your spiritual reserves. Why let guilt feelings jinx you. Divine love does not ask questions.

How do you react in danger? Know, and plan constructively with your natural tendencies. Psychic retaliation: feasible? Yes. Ethical? Usually. Worthwhile or necessary? Not always. Biblical "quotations" if adopted should be taken in context. "Turning the other cheek" belongs with "blessing them that hate you." The great spiritual potency of blessing. Stopping an exchange of injuries. "Astral rebound" not always deliberately caused, but can be a natural result of freeing a victim from an obsessing image.

Psychic self-defense—a normal part of healthy living.
Don't live in the past—move on into your new bright
future.

How an enterprise needs psychic self-defense. Giving your
project an auspicious beginning. Endowing the growing
venture with its own protective aura. Vital psychic creativity to aid any enterprise. Ongoing vision, ongoing action.

Material and psychic action both needed against crime.
The "Claiming Techniques: its timeless magical power to
protect your treasures. Joint psychic defense with your
neighbors. Transforming children and seniors from being
potential victims. Psychically cleansing the locality. Social
and spiritual aspects of psychic defense against crime.

Definitions and comments upon psychological and other
terms used in this book.

Introduction

Psychic self-defense—it sounds like there is a war going on, and that people need to defend themselves against the invading hordes!

Well, in a very big sense, it is true.

There is a "war" going on—not the kind of war we fear most, with soldiers and missiles, spies and counterspies, and secret new weapons—but a never-ending war of words, appeals, noise, stimulation . . . and of psychic missiles and psychological weapons. (And maybe there is a little bit of psychic espionage going on.)

Only a part of this war is openly "declared" by those who seek to sell you things you don't need, services you really don't want, and investments you can't afford, or who wish to gain your vote or support, or your "tax deductible gift." Much of this war is just "there" as part of our modern bureaucratic and industrial culture, but it is nevertheless, despite the good intentions of "socially responsible" government and business, undermining you as the person you want to be and should become.

Psychic self-defense is not a matter of burdensome armor or the constant exercise of countermeasures. It is not walking in constant fear of attack, suspecting a lurker at every threshold. Rather, is it a matter of strength, of confidence, of success and fulfillment coming to you through the employment of some simple and perfectly natural psychic techniques.

Some people do these things quite naturally and instinctively, without knowing anything about the principles or techniques used in this book. But others have been conditioned, falsely, not to use these natural powers, or they have lost these instinctive abilities through some early psychic injuries unknowingly sustained in this invisible war.

Offense is the best defense! You have heard that before, but here it takes on an altogether new meaning: the principles and techniques you will learn in these pages can make you strong, poised, free from enslavement to others' desires, confident in your own self, expressing and living your own true beliefs, and happy and successful in your own work. It's not really "armed preparedness"—being ready to shoot off your own psychic missiles if any attacker looks as if he might launch his own. Better to call it "free-dom through strength."

It's like health. When you build solid health through good nutrition, exercise, a clean environment, and sound habits, you don't have to live in fear of drafts from open windows, or contamination from sick people, or contact with the natural world around you. Instead, the strength of good health gives you natural resistance to ill-health.

And, in fact, the principles of psychic self-defense will also contribute to your physical health, for there is indeed a tie between the psyche and the physical body, and employment of the techniques taught in this book will result in well-being.

But this book does not avoid or skim over the very real possibility that you may have specific needs for defense against direct psychic attack.

There is a lot of nonsense about the occult written and produced in books and magazines, on radio and television, and most especially in the movies. There is just as much nonsense about the occult coming from generally well-intentioned ministers, doctors, teachers and ordinary people. It is mostly nonsense because most of it is based on fiction, superstition, misinformation, and even deliberate falsehood.

Some of it has nothing at all to do with the occult. Instead, it relates to people who are sick, or criminal, or even insane who have called themselves "occultists" as a cover for what they are really doing, or why they are doing it.

But even nonsense can be dangerous if it induces fear or incorrect action. No "ghost" ever hurt anyone—but fear of such an entity has caused people to have accidents, some of them fatal. It is the same situation as with a hallucination—what is hallucinated isn't "there," but the illusion that it is there can bring about the same consequences as if it were. People have died of fright, or have become sick, or have had accidents, or lost friends or possessions, or have in turn brought injury to others as the result of seeing, or believing in, what is later found to be an illusion.

And, psychically, fear, or belief in something, can invite psychic and even physical injury. Belief in a curse can make that curse powerful and real. Belief in someone's "power" adds to that power, and if enough people believe in that power it can even grow to dominate the person who supposedly possessed it: "absolute power corrupts absolutely."

That famous quotation came from a letter written by Lord Acton to Bishop Creighton in 1887. But John Milton, two centuries earlier, wrote:

> Some say no evil thing that walks by night,
> In fog or fire, by lake or moorish fen,
> Blue meagre hag, or stubborn unlaid ghost,
> That breaks his magic chains at curfew time,
> No goblin, or swart faery of the mine,
> Hath hurtful power o'er true virginity.

In the lore of magick, there has been a great deal written and said about the remarkable powers of the "virgin" (boy or girl) to overcome evil or to give strength to the good. But it is not the familiar definition of "virgin" as a person who has not experienced sexual intercourse that is meant in this lore—rather we mean one whose "purity of character" is such as to perceive the world only truly and without invitation to false interpretation or experience. Such a virgin has all his or her natural psychic defenses in place.

Correct knowledge can also protect you from false perception of the world around you, and free you from reacting to illusions that can bring harm, just as in the example of the person whose fear of ghosts led to an accident.

This book will give you a great deal of "correct knowledge" about the occult, and in the process straighten out a lot of the nonsense mentioned earlier that has led many naïve people to walk in fear of demons and curses, of possession and jinxes, and denied to them their own natural psychic talents that would protect them from the rare, real psychic attack and the more general psychic warfare polluting our mental and psychic space nowadays.

"Correct knowledge" about the occult is definitely one of our reasons for publishing this book, not only to correct the nonsense and superstition so common as a result of mass entertainment and evangelical demagoguery, but also to make genuine occultism more acceptable to the psychologist, the minister, the doctor, and others who could find in these principles and time-proven techniques much of value to their own fields.

Modern holistic medicine is much more open today to nonmaterial possibilities, but discoveries being made about the psychic side of disease could be far greater if it was more generally known that Western occultism was much more sophisticated than is generally presumed.

We cannot expect modern business to turn off the psychic pollution anymore than we can reasonably expect air pollution to stop overnight. But we can equip everyone with a good psychic self-defense system, and in doing so we expect to see an improvement in the psychic atmosphere as well. Each step along the way can enable more "clear thinking" people to then apply themselves to some of the other problems facing our civilization—including real air pollution, the abuse of the natural environment, and the dangers of real warfare.

—Carl Llewellyn Weschcke
Publisher

1

Why Psychic
Self-Defense?

Study Points

1. Psychic self-defense is vital to every person.

2. Each person is a composite of body, feeling, mind, and spirit all ceaselessly interacting with each other.

   a. It is the *astral level*—the instinctual functions of the body's nervous systems together with the emotional functions—that is the most vulnerable to psychic influences.

1

b. The imagination is a special function of the astral level of the psyche, and the imagination can be skillfully directed by the rational mind to picture that which is good for the whole person.

c. Things of which we are not conscious can affect us through the astral level: things forgotten or repressed, things perceived subliminally, things that reach us purely as astral.

3. Just as each person's physical body is part of the physical world, so each person's astral level is part of the astral world.

a. Conscious action can be induced from unconscious experience—such as subliminal advertising of which we remain unaware, and which influences us to make irrational decisions.

b. The astral level, both of the psyche and of the world, is the meeting place of influences from the physical, instinctual, emotional, mental, and spiritual activity of purely natural phenomena, other human beings, and other beings.

c. While all these activities can influence us, they need not—for we have natural defenses within which we live and move, and we can make these defenses stronger.

    d. It is through the astral level that deliberate or sometimes unintended psychic attacks or the psychic effects of jealousy, anger, or attempts to dominate us reach us.

4. Sometimes, through sickness or from emotional causes, our natural defense (our "resistance") is lowered; some people are just naturally more open to certain influences; some activities make us more open.

5. For true psychic self-defense a well-fortified aura is the basic need.

    a. "Sensitives" and psychics need techniques of aura fortification to "switch off" their openness.

    b. People in the business world are particularly subject to forms of psychic stress.

    c. People involved in welfare work or in counseling are likewise subjected to particular kinds of psychic stress.

    d. Any physically or emotionally sick person will benefit from aura fortification.

    e. The stay-at-home parent needs psychic self-defense: the stay-at-home parent is the center of the family's demands; as the chief buyer for the family, the stay-at-home parent is subjected to the advertising and sales pressures of the total consumption-oriented economy.

• • •

Psychic self-defense concerns *you*. It merits the attention of every intelligent human being. It has a vital part to fulfill: in our duty toward ourselves, in our responsibility toward our dear ones and toward all who may be in our care, and in our responsibility to society and to the biosphere as a whole. Psychic self-defense is important in our physical and emotional, and even in our mental and spiritual well-being, because each person is a composite of physical, emotional, mental, and spiritual levels that ceaselessly interact with each other.

The level of this composite that is most directly vulnerable to psychic influence comprises the lowest, instinctual functions of the psyche (that enmesh with the bodily nervous system) together with the emotional functions. These latter are linked, below, with the instincts and extend, above, into rationally directed or even spiritually charged emotions. The whole range we term the astral level of the psyche; some writers term its lower portions the etheric, but for our purposes it is more suitable to consider them as one.

The imagination is a special function of the astral level of the psyche. It is liable to be colored by impulses arising from the instincts and the bodily senses, such as those of sex or of hunger; equally, it can be skillfully directed by the rational mind to picture that which is seen to be good for the whole person. It can even image forth in its own manner the high aspirations of a person's spiritual nature.

We are not conscious of every function of the psyche, such as, for example, that which directs digestion. But the psyche certainly has these functions, as we can tell when worry upsets someone's stomach, or an "out-pouring" of long-buried memories produces diarrhea. Unfortunately, too, we may not know what made us do or made us say something on impulse. Such problems arise because, besides those concerns that the psyche can handle very well without our conscious attention, there are other concerns that we have swept under the carpet.

Problems arising from the burial in the unconscious of material that is really not in its province are partly caused by personal attitudes, usually by an unreadiness to cope emotionally with a situation when it arises (say during one's childhood or during a period of general stress), and a failure to review it later when greater maturity or equilibrium, or wider knowledge, could be brought to it. Frequently, however, problems are caused by attitudes that seem built into our society rather than being personal in nature. For a number of people, the state of things is improving, but there are still many for whom various aspects of death, of sex, of even ordinary bodily functions, are not only not to be "talked about"—it is not the question of public utterance that matters—but are not to be recognized, even in thought, as a part of life. Even one's own emotions, or perceptions of plain facts, are not to be privately admitted if they do not conform to an imaginary "standard pattern."

The result of such a condition can easily be that our conscious mind is no longer aware of many matters that do in fact concern it, while our unconscious mind experiences the sensation of being burdened, guilty, and fearful over troubles that it can neither comprehend nor deal with.

It is a good thing for all of us from time to time to look back over the past, not to brood, but to bring it as far as we can into the light of our present knowledge and understanding.

In the external universe that is all around us, there is also an "astral world" of which each person's own astral level is a part; just as there is a material world of which each person's physical body is a part, an intellectual world of which each person's mind is a part, and a spiritual world of which each person's spirit is a part.

The fact that we are quite unconscious of much that goes on at these various levels, both outside and inside ourselves, does not make our position more secure, but quite the reverse. To illustrate this, recall the publicity that was given some years back to the subject of subliminal advertising.

The word subliminal means, literally, "below the threshold"; in this case "below the threshold of consciousness," and therefore "not within conscious awareness." Back in the seventeenth century, the philosopher Leibniz observed that perceptions which were too slight, or too transient, to be consciously noticed might still be perceived unconsciously, and these unconscious perceptions might, then or at a later time, stimulate conscious imaginings, thoughts, words, or deeds, still without coming to consciousness themselves. They remained "subliminal."

As an example: A person living in an old house, which as long as he has known it has had cracks in the plaster and creaking boards in the floors, may never consciously have estimated the extent of either the cracks or the creaks.

Consciously, therefore, he does not perceive that both are gradually becoming more serious; if there are material advantages in living there, he may not even be willing to see the deterioration. But something in the unconscious part of his psyche has paid heed to the matter, and ultimately he begins to have dreams about the place collapsing.

If he is too clever, he will label these as insecurity dreams, and may go on living there until the house really does collapse. If he is not clever enough, he will ignore the dreams completely, with exactly the same result. If, however, he has an average mind—he is likely to let the dream draw his attention to the facts, and call in a surveyor. He is then likely, however, to decide that the timely warning in his dream was a special bonus from heaven. This is not surprising, because at no time is he likely to remember noticing the deterioration from which his unconscious mind formulated the warning.

This peculiar ability of the psyche to produce conscious action from unconscious experience began to be exploited in advertising some years back. One method took the form of inserting in a cinematic film a few frames conveying the intended message. What the subject of the film as a whole might be was unimportant. When the film was shown, the conscious mind of a viewer could not possibly detect the passing of the implanted frames as more than the merest flicker, and normally would not register the frames at all, but the unconscious mind, which is part of the nonrational area of the psyche, got the message. Furthermore, this message was almost certain to be acted upon, because the rational mind, having no awareness of the transaction, could form no judgment about it. The effect was very much like that of a post-hypnotic suggestion.

In an experiment conducted to demonstrate the method, a film on a neutral subject was prepared by inserting in it a few frames illustrating a soft drink, This film was shown to a volunteer audience of men and women of various ages and lifestyles. After the showing, attendants moved around with trays of assorted drinks, and an overwhelming majority of the audience chose the one that had been subliminally shown.

This type of advertising has, rightly, been adjudged an infringement of personal liberties. But what, then, becomes of the liberty of the individual when other subtle forces of fear, desire, stimulation, or depression play unperceived upon the psyche?

Such subtle forces may be produced deliberately or accidentally with or without malice, and with or without understanding. They are usually caused by human beings, but sometimes they are of nonhuman origin. Sometimes their victims are their unknowing originators.

The astral level, both in the psyche and in the surrounding environment, is in fact the meeting place of innumerable influences that originate from the physical, instinctual, emotional, mental, and spiritual activity of human beings and other beings. Natural phenomena such as earthquakes and electrical storms, specific message-givers such as colors, sounds, and odors, and various manmade energy sources, too, all produce subtle as well as obvious vibrations. All contribute their share to the ever-varying barrage of astral influences. The uncanny forecasts of those people who possess an "earthquake aura," the heightened cognition often shown by sailors, forestry workers, pilots, and others who live in relationship to natural forces, indicate the existence of influences that are present for all of us, whether we know of them or not, whether we become conscious of them or not.

Occult activity also, if undertaken without due knowledge and care, can open dangerous doorways to powerful forces that may affect other people besides the operator.

Besides this, in some cases, the possibility of occult action deliberately aimed to influence a person's deeds, emotions, or health, even when well meant, may not turn out well if skill, understanding, and the subject's free consent are lacking. (It is a sound occult principle to require the subject's permission, even for distant healing.)

We are not at the mercy of *all* these influences; we are not at the mercy of any of them if we are within the normal range of physical and psychic health.

We all have natural defenses within which we live and move, and we can use natural means to make these defenses stronger yet.

Sometimes, however, through sickness or from emotional causes, our resistance may be lowered. Some of us are especially at risk with regard to particular types of influences. All of us need to know the insidious dangers, the symptoms, the protective and the remedial measures to adopt, for specific kinds of psychic attack.

The present book gives facts, advice, and practices that ought to be known to everyone, while at the same time dealing with the specialized needs of particular types of people.

Who are the people whose special needs have to be taken into consideration? Not all the specific problems dealt with in this book can be listed here, but among the people who should pay particular heed to psychic self-defense we can mention the following:

The occultist needs to be careful. Traditionally, the older style occult orders have long indulged in a certain amount of "feuding" among themselves, such as can be glimpsed in the writings of Aleister Crowley and even of Dion Fortune. It is a foolish tradition we can well dispense with, and in these busy times most of us are fully occupied without such pranks. However, there are undoubtedly occasions when an occultist does incur the anger or the jealousy of his (or her) kind, and they are likely to make their feelings known, if they can, by some form of retaliation which bears the signature of their art.

One night in recent years, a young occultist who was astrally attacked while asleep by an opponent of this sort, succeeded easily in warding off the attack and dismissing the assailant; but in the morning a large piece of furniture in the same room was found to be dented as if with many blows, similar to those that had failed to harm the intended victim. This was a curious phenomenon, and it can only be supposed that the thwarted assailant, in departing, left the marks to prove his attack was real.

This type of aggression is a different matter from the assaults by lower elementals that are referred to in *Practical*

Guide to Astral Projection. Those assaults generally are only the result of a chance meeting, in which case evasive action is all that is likely to be required. Hauntings, again, do not in most cases involve any form of attack (a comforting thought for nervous people), but different types of haunting will be discussed later in this book.

For true self-defense in psychic matters, a well-fortified aura is a basic need, and in the next chapter we shall discuss the nature and maintenance of this.

The powerful shield of the aura is likewise of great importance in withstanding a quite different kind of attack which may beset the occultist, the mystic, or any original thinker. Especially in his (or her) younger days, there may be trouble from opposing forces set in motion by non-occult, nonmystical people, most often by alarmed or indignant relatives, friends, or neighbors. Despite their lack of knowledge, they may collectively generate a considerable amount of emotional opposition against the rebel's work, beliefs, or lifestyle, and while they are fully entitled to defend themselves against something they feel to be a threat to their traditional views, any weakness on the part of the person making the new beginning could turn the "clan's" self-defense into a destructive attack whether intended or not. Such a situation has to be recognized, and faced with resolution.

An exact picture of this kind of opposition can be found in the Gospel of Mark, the first portion of chapter 6. The passage concludes with these words:

But Jesus said unto them, "A prophet is unhonored only in his own region, and among his own kinsfolk, and in his own home." And there he could do no great work, except to lay his hands upon a few sick people and heal them. And he marveled at their unbelief.

It is noteworthy here, since we are considering psychic self-defense techniques, that the responsibility for this local lack of success is put back formally where it belongs: and he marveled at their unbelief.

It is rather fashionable lately, when any matters hinging on relationships do not go forward as we wish, to be endlessly asking ourselves, "How have I failed?" and then quite likely to fail also to find a reply. Certainly, we should take complete responsibility for our own actions whether good, bad, or mistaken. Such taking of responsibility strengthens our defenses both astrally and spiritually, but letting other people make us feel culpable when we are not at fault is entirely different, and can shatter every defense we have.

Another group of people, whose needs in psychic self-defense are, in a way, specialized, are the sensitives, the mediums, and everyone else who is popularly described as "psychic." Many people who in adolescence or adulthood have chosen to become magicians, occultists, or healers actively directing the forces of the nonmaterial world, start off as sensitives and owe their later preoccupations to their passive childhood experience of nonmaterial realities. Other sensitives, however, by reason of their temperament or their beliefs, find their life's work in further developing and employing their receptive faculties in clairvoyance, divination, prophecy, and mediumship. The meaning of the term sensitive is plain. If such a person is deeply disturbed while looking into a murder or suicide, for instance, or is nauseated by some quite normal contact with commercial life, none need wonder.

A sensitive cannot in fact be other than sensitive.

What the medium, the clairvoyant, and the other gifted people in this category need to do (and what, if they have been trained by a teacher, they should have learned to do), in order to make life livable for themselves and their associates, is to switch off their nonmaterial perceptions when these are not positively required. Those who have been naturally "psychic" from childhood and have not gone into active occultism are the ones most likely to have missed being taught to "switch off," so we are exploring something about this in the next chapter.

Having mentioned the world of commerce, and of business life, we can indicate the special reasons why psychic self-defense is necessary to the men and women whose working career is encompassed within that framework. The fact that people can survive and frequently even prosper in its atmosphere does not constitute evidence that it is particularly healthful to the psyche. The most successful people generally have hobbies and avocations vastly different from their working activities. While even the least perceptive workers sometimes become at least semiconscious of the continual barrage of inquisitiveness, envy, ambitions, jealousies, and rivalries at every level in business that ceaselessly tries, tests, challenges, leans on, steps on, saps, crushes, buys, sells, or otherwise seeks to profit by any human being within the walls. This may not be quite universal, but is endemic in the atmosphere of most large business concerns.

In such a charged atmosphere, the effects of any additional stresses are multiplied disproportionately. Additional stresses usually are added from time to time by the power-trips and ego-trips of individuals spurred by the sight of some coveted goal or by some motivation internal to themselves: besides the simply ambitious there is often a sprinkling of compulsive achievers and neurotics with a need to be needed, with whom no normally hard-working person could possibly compete.

Apart from pressure at the conscious level by these hypercompetitive attitudes, there has to be taken into consideration what most people mean by "atmosphere," the collective psyche-to-psyche communication that is really at the subliminal level. Its effects emerge into consciousness as irrational anxiety, stress, anger, seemingly causeless impulses of aggression or of fear, and in some people of depression and feelings of inferiority. None of these destructive emotional reactions, of course, are limited to people who stand in the line-of-advance of the "trippers"; they will affect anyone within range whose psychic defenses are below par.

A very large and widely assorted group of people, to whom an understanding of psychic self-defense is essential besides their other skills, consists of those whose daily work brings them into contact with the psychic needs of others, whether at the spiritual, emotional, or instinctual level. Such people are welfare workers, probation officers, nurses (especially in mental nursing), psychotherapists, counselors, clergy, and all who are often in the company of disturbed or erratic folk. The effects of continual contact, both conscious and subliminal, with the negative or disproportional emotional attitudes of those who are being helped can sometimes be very considerable. Professional helpers (clergy or therapists, for example) are normally taught some defense techniques as part of their training, but this is not invariably so; and many generous givers may not realize the necessity for self-protection.

Besides being essential to their own welfare and continued capacity for service (an avoidance of the sudden breakdowns, attacks of shingles, and other ills that beset the psychically poisoned or depleted), reflection upon their own need for defense will help them understand more vividly the reality of the forces with which the sufferers are contending. And it is supremely important that they should understand this reality. This, indeed, is one of the reasons why intending givers of psychic aid to others, whether as psychiatrists, therapists, or clergy, should themselves receive analysis as part of their training: that they may experience consciously something of the worlds that lie, for each of us, beyond the comfortable "four walls, roof, and floor" of rationality. They will be better able to give aid, and they will safeguard their own well-being.

It seems like a needless truism to say that the psychically sick themselves are in need of psychic self-defense, but there are some aspects of this that may be less obvious than would appear at first glance. Any sick person, whether the psyche or the body seems to be the main focus of sickness, is in need of psychic self-defense, and not only for the treatment of the malady with which they are said to be afflicted.

Certainly, with regard to a specific malady, psychic self-defense is often a means to considerable benefit, sometimes even to a cure. There is no dichotomy between the psyche and the physical body: a person is one unit. Sufferers have, however, another need for help, too: throughout the natural world (of which we are indissolubly a part), it is most often the sick, weak, or injured creatures that are preyed upon by others. When lions pursue a herd of antelope, it is not the finest and strongest that is taken; the lions hang on to see which animal will fall behind the fast-moving body of the herd, to find the one that tires or stumbles first. At the other end of the scale of predators, although medical science can point to this or that bacillus, this or that virus, as the cause of a particular disease, it is becoming well recognized that such agents of infection are present in even the healthiest people. What induces disease by allowing the multiplication of these organisms may be a chill, shock, malnutrition, depression, a sense of rejection, or any other negative state. Likewise, the unseen worlds are full of influences and of beings that are drawn to a flow of uncontrolled psychic energy. It behooves us, therefore, to protect both the psychically and the physically infirm.

An understanding of psychic self-defense is often needed, too, within the framework of family relationships. This is not necessarily a question of such blatant cases as battered wives or henpecked husbands, but of a very general and rather subtle misuse of the concepts of love and harmony.

The overprotected person, whether spouse, child (even when adult), or, often, parent or other senior relative, may be unable to make a stand against some perhaps heartbreaking frustration, either because they are simply denied privacy and opportunity, or because they are made to feel it would "hurt" or "annoy" others.

Paradoxically, misuse of love occurs when every member of a family plays this kind of power-game, on varying terms, with the rest.

If only one person in such a situation regains his or her psychic integrity, a way may be found to release all the players, making family life what it should be: a way to each member's self-fulfillment, and to help in attainment of personal goals.

Quite apart from any possible domestic stresses, however, the stay-at-home parent in a special way needs knowledge of psychic self-defense.

The stay-at-home parent may not at first see why relationships with spouse, relatives, children, and children's teachers may not be everything the stay-at-home parent could wish. Quite likely, he or she has never been concerned with occult matters, and the idea that anyone might want to attack his or her psychic integrity is absurd.

What motive could anyone have?

A very plain one. Usually, apart from big occasional purchases, the stay-at-home parent is the family's chief buyer. Unique though he or she is as a person, to the marketers of foods, clothing, cleaning materials, and household wares the stay-at-home parent is as one herring in a shoal to the fisherman: not by any means an object of personal malice, but fair game if permitted to be caught.

Does he or she behave like the herring, or like the intelligent person the stay-at-home parent really is? Only the stay-at-home parent can know.

If he or she frequently comes home from the supermarket with items he or she did not mean to buy, that is a danger sign. (If she or her family really has no use for those items, that's an even bigger danger sign.)

If he or she dreads agents and salespeople calling, not just because they could be intruders in disguise, but because the stay-at-home parent knows he or she could be pressured into buying something unwanted, or even just because he or she will let them waste precious time, that's another danger sign.

If the stay-at-home parent cannot pinpoint any of these things but somehow never quite knows where the housekeeping money goes—danger again!

Many of the pitfalls that beset the stay-at-home parent when buying the groceries will beset both the stay-at-home parent and working spouse in a rather different guise when they go to buy a house or a car, or to rent accommodations for a vacation.

Such pitfalls are simply psychic (or psychological if you prefer): that is, they involve instinctual and emotional reactions of which people may be only partially aware, and when they do become aware, they may not know how to act.

The truth is that our material civilization, while in many ways having increased our need for psychic protection, has also done much to deprive us of those means of self-defense that should be naturally and rightfully ours.

The pressures upon us have increased to an almost unbelievable extent. Of course, it concerns us to know what is going on in the Middle East, in the Far East, in South America, Africa, and Europe. It may concern us to know what happens in the stock markets of some other countries. A relatively short time back (as human evolution goes) we physically could not have known all these things, even where our present subjects of concern then existed. Now we can not only hear the news items, we can see them, in our own home, and often within an hour or so of their happening: elections, fires, cataclysms, legal processes, revolutions, everything.

Of course, all this helps make us citizens of the world, and it develops our understanding of affairs. There is no need to regret this new information. It does, however, greatly increase the range of material that comes into the life-experience of each man and each woman; it can in some ways greatly increase our anxieties, our emotional involvement; and, since the events are not really happening in our living room and we can do nothing whatever about them, it must often increase the level of our daily feelings of stress, tension, and frustration. For this reason, many aware and sensitive people deliberately ration themselves to one news broadcast every twenty-four hours.

Then there are people you meet who invite you to their church or their club. If you really want to go, that's fine. You may, however, feel you do not want to go and yet do not like to refuse: they are nice friendly people and so insistent! Do you refuse, and feel guilty and ashamed and avoid them ever after? Or do you go, and feel guilty and ashamed because it is not "you"? Either way, you may feel you have lost a bit of yourself, a bit of your control over your own life.

Do you sometimes suspect that if your own defenses were what they should be, other people would not be able to make you do things you do not want?

A person of any type can have first-rate psychic defenses; the effect varies with personality and circumstances. Everyone knows the rugged extrovert who "is never pushed around." You may have heard of, or even met with, people of a different sort—frequently quiet and reserved—who can, for instance, order rats or mice out of their dwelling and be obeyed. Again, you encounter people who are always relaxed, easy in manner, natural in any situation. What strikes you about all these people is that they are *so natural*. It's the people with poor defenses who are awkward, uncertain what to do, and unsure of themselves.

In this book, the basic principles and most important methods of psychic self-defense are explained so you can master them and adapt them to your own needs. Some of the examples we have mentioned may have struck you as being particularly related to your experience; or you may wish to develop all your natural inner powers as far as you can, and you realize psychic self-defense is an essential part of that program. Or you may feel simply that you are more vulnerable than you should be to psychic attack, frequently imposed on, jangled with rush and noise, "missing a skin," or just plain unlucky.

In any of these cases, there is real help for you here. Not only are these principles and techniques of psychic self-defense of high value individually; beyond that, the cumulative strengthening of the psyche will help you build true self-knowledge, confidence, and character. That is the great defense.

· · ·

Checkpoint

- Psychic self-defense concerns you. Consider this chapter carefully, point by point, and see where you fit in.

- Do any of the descriptions of different people's needs fit you or your life? In any case, do not ignore all the rest. Psychic self-defense is mainly a matter of basic human nature.

2

Forcefields and Power Sources

Study Points

1. Your prime need in psychic self-defense is for a well-fortified aura.

2. There are two main divisions to the aura:

   a. The alpha forcefield, or electrical aura, radiated by the physical body.

   b. The beta forcefield or psychic aura: an emanation of energy from the total personality that is radiated by the astral body.

3. In *Practical Guide to Psychic Self-Defense* our concern is with the beta forcefield, for when the psyche is infused with energy of a high spiritual vibration, the aura becomes a protective barrier that effectively excludes all external yetziratic (astral) forces of a lower vibration than its own.

   a. The power of the spiritually developed psychic aura can extend far beyond the physical body.

   b. This aura, with right thinking and practice, prevents the approach of any non-material entities, unless you give permission. This continues whether you are awake or asleep.

   c. Destructive atmospheres will also be deflected by the well-developed psychic aura.

   d. The well-developed psychic aura will also deflect many mundane disturbances—such as door-to-door salespeople, beggars, time-wasters, pollsters, etc.

   e. Even material actions may be deflected by a powerful aura, giving protection against physical harm in situations of violence, accidents, natural disasters, and even contagious diseases.

4. A well-developed aura also increases your well-being, confidence, courage, etc., and the respect others will have for you. It also leads to greater self-fulfillment.

5. The protective psychic aura can be damaged from within by these three kinds of fear:

   a. **Rational fear**—which is based on a true knowledge of the facts, and that can be met by rationally determined actions.

   b. **Habitual (irrational) fear**—which is usually out of proportion to the real facts, and that may be based on some real event of the past (such as an accident happening in childhood) or something that vividly stimulated the imagination (such as a frightening story). It can usually be overcome by restoring the feared object or event to its proper proportion through rational analysis, or remembrance of the actual circumstances, or by relaxation of the aroused tension and diversion of the attention.

   c. **Sudden fear**—which may be caused by subliminal influences, in other words, it may be a correct reaction to unconscious perceptions. It may make its appearance in dreams. Sensitivity to all levels of our being can bring a proper resolution to these fears. And, relating to the higher self provides a center of strength and true sense of values to bring balance and discrimination to your decisions.

6. Conscious contact with your higher self is:

   a. Your contact with the divine mind, of which the higher self is a spark.

   b. Your contact with the ideal you are designed to become.

   c. Your contact with inexhaustible divine blessing.

· · ·

Your prime need in psychic self-defense is a well-fortified aura. In this chapter, therefore, we must consider what the aura is, and then how it is to be strengthened.

Some confusion has arisen in the past, and is continued by various writers, as to whether in referring to the aura a very fine material manifestation is meant, or a dense astral one. Each is possible, for there are two main divisions of the aura. As stated in *The Magical Philosophy*:

"Associated with the astral body is the aura (cf. Book III, pp. 220–201), an emanation of energy from the total personality that is radiated by the astral body; it is technically referred to as the beta forcefield, its physical counterpart being the electrical aura or alpha forcefield, which is radiated by the physical organism. Many phenomena commonly held to be of psychic origin are in fact produced by the electrical aura ... In this series, the term "aura" is used to designate the beta forcefield ... When the psyche is infused with energy of a high spiritual vibration, the aura (or the Argyraigis, to give it its esoteric title in this circumstance) becomes a protective barrier which effectively excludes all external Yetziratic [astral] forces of a lower vibration than its own." ("The Triumph of Light" pages 40–41.)

A classic study of the alpha forcefield, that is the electrical aura, studied and measured by physical means, is *The Human Aura** by Walter J. Kilner, the physician whose researches led after his death, to the development of the well-known "Kilner goggles" that enable many people to see the electrical aura. In *The Human Aura* he gives a great

---

*Reprinted 1965 with a foreword by Leslie Shephard, University Books (New York).

number of case histories, carefully described, with classifications and illustrations of the electrical aura as affected by some conditions of health. Although psychological knowledge was very limited in his day, this book remains of considerable interest to the student of the aura's relationship to bodily health.

Our concern, however, is with the beta forcefield, or psychic aura. In reality, the two forcefields are not disunited, just as a person's astral and physical bodies are not disunited; but they are distinct in nature and purpose. Some manifestations of the psychic aura are so close to the physical that the ability to see them is no guarantee of other forms of clairvoyance; but should there be any doubt as to which aura is being perceived, the psychic aura can usually be distinguished at once by its greater brilliance, brighter colors, and swifter variance with emotional or spiritual conditions. It is also a less precise mirror of the physical health of the subject. This is not to deny that some psychic auras can be seen that have muddy colors, with a lack of movement or of luminousness; but in such cases the whole character of the subject will be in accord with those qualities, so the seer need not be perplexed.

Children fairly frequently see the psychic aura of the people around them, and surround their drawings of people with bright patches of yellow, blue, red, or green without any awareness of being unconventional.

In adult art, two facts have influenced the conditions in which the aura may be represented, or partly represented. One fact is that the more highly developed a person's spirituality, the more brilliant will be the aura, and consequently the greater the number of clairvoyants who will be able to see it. In extreme instances, the brilliance will be perceived in the physical aura too. The other fact is that the intensity of brilliance is likely to be greatest and most visible around the head. This has led to the convention of representing the whole aura, or simply the portion surrounding the head, solely to characterize divine or saintly figures in both Eastern and Western art.

The nimbus or halo surrounding the head is familiar in religious art in one form or another, down to modern times; the "glory" surrounding the whole figure has become less familiar in the West. Chinese sculpture from about the sixth century C.E., perhaps as a result of Nestorian or Manichee influence, shows the Buddha and other high beings with a circular or leaf-shaped halo, or with a full-figure "glory" usually leaf-shaped. In the Middle Ages the "glory" came via Byzantium into Italian art, in which it was popularly called a "mandorla." (Not to be confused with mandala; a mandorla is so named from being shaped like an almond, the broad end—the area of greatest luminosity—being around the head of the figure.) With the Renaissance, however, and the new preoccupation with the material world, the full-figure glory or mandorla went out of fashion in Western art, though the halo became more realistic.

In real life, however, the power of a spiritually developed psychic aura can extend far beyond a person's physical presence. This is not a matter of speculation, nor of hearsay about people renowned for sanctity. It is a matter of experience among people who take their inner life seriously.

The Magical Philosophy recounts the history of a young woman named Laura who, while in a state of conscious projection from her physical body, called on a male friend in order to see what ailed him and to perform a healing. She arrived astrally in his home, but found herself unable to approach within a considerable distance of him until she had brought clearly to mind her purpose in doing so. The story as there given is meant chiefly to demonstrate Laura's experience; but it will be interesting now to consider the same episode as it relates to the man concerned.

John E. was an initiate of considerable stature, whose troubles had largely been caused by the impact upon his life of serious external events.

After having committed himself to a career of inner development and spiritual endeavor, he was called up for military service. His first thought was to register as a conscientious objector, and this in his case would have been a true declaration; but as it happened, while he was awaiting his turn to be interviewed, he was left in an anteroom with a few young men who were going to make the same declaration for altogether selfish and debased reasons, and who assumed he was another like themselves.

Their talk so revolted him that when his name was called he went in and told the examining officials that he had changed his mind. He would agree to do military service if he could be kept on noncombatant duties. Accordingly, he became a P.I. instructor.

This struggle and compromise with his conscience is mentioned because the inward tensions set up were very likely involved in the sequel. After about a year of army work which, as far as he was aware, he found absorbing and worthwhile, he was one day giving a demonstration of running uphill carrying a heavy gun, when he slipped and suffered internal injuries which included a torn aorta.

The treatment he received was effective for most of his injuries, but the damaged main artery continued to be troublesome, and when as a consequence he was invalided out of the army, it looked as if he would have to indefinitely dose himself with medicine to relieve the strain on the cardiac muscles, albeit with sideeffects that could undermine his once excellent general health.

When, in his subsequent civilian work, he met Laura, he told her nothing of his personal troubles save that he had a health problem that sometimes impaired his working abilities. Nor did he tell her that he at once recognized her as one whose greatest potential, as yet unperceived by herself, lay in the inward life; but he used every conversation between them to broaden and deepen her understanding of occult and mystical matters. He did not fall in love with her, and she on her side fell in love, not with him, but with the ideals—her own ideals—which he made clear to her. She was correspondingly grateful.

That is the background for the episode in which Laura, who had from childhood been an occasional astral traveler, set out astrally one night to discover what his injury was, and, if possible, to heal it. Had he been a man of only average psychic development, she assuredly could have entered his presence without difficulty; as it was, as soon as she touched the outer edge of his aura she felt she could move no further in that direction.

He, meanwhile, awoke from sleep and perceived the astral intrusion. Becoming aware of Laura's identity and, now, her declared purpose, he silently bade her approach and thus opened the way for her. But still she tells us "it was like going through a fine-mesh sieve." She felt sifted, refined, purified, by passing through his aura, so powerful was it.

Her side of the story, and its good outcome, is told and examined in "The Triumph of Light" (Book IV of *The Magical Philosophy*) pages 29–35; it is also further analyzed in *Practical Guide to Astral Projection*.

Your aura, too, with right thinking and practice, has the power to absolutely prevent the approach of nonmaterial entities without your leave. Whether you are awake or asleep, no astral vampire, no incubus or succubus or other nonmaterial intruder can pierce the shield of a developed psychic aura.

Destructive, nerve-sapping atmospheres also will be deflected from you by this natural defense.

Nor are these psychic benefits the only ones you will receive from a well-developed and intact aura. A frequent and well-attested result of this development is that the person ceases noticeably to be pestered by street vendors, beggars and the like, or in situations that were previously troublesome. The reason is that these folk are usually highly perceptive in their own fashion; they have to be, and they have no wish to waste their time on someone with whom they do not "feel" they will succeed. You will cease, in fact, to wear your kind heart "on your sleeve."

Do you find people argue with you whenever you express an opinion or a purpose? Do you have only to mention a wish or a view, and a relative or workmate will try to persuade you that you ought to think differently? When you have rightly developed your aura, most of this attempted interference will stop, and the rest of it will cease to cause you any concern. To say it will leave you untouched like water off a duck's back is a quaint description of the way any sort of aggressiveness will slide off your protective aura.

It is difficult to find an adequate image for this in the human world. St. Paul's well-known metaphor about "putting on the whole armor of God" is generally acceptable; the wearing of armor, though admittedly something artificial to human beings, has been familiar in many forms throughout history. The shining shield of your aura, however, is a natural part of your own being.

It is no more "put on" than the bright eyes and glowing skin of physical health are "put on." Like those physical attributes, it grows from within; and while the awareness of it will certainly give you good courage, your aura will also become stronger still as your courage increases.

One phrase in that passage from the Epistle to the Ephesians is noteworthy for us: "taking, besides, the shield of faith, with which you will be able to quell all the burning darts of the wicked" (Ephesians 6:16).

In other words, do not question if this will work. Do not wonder whether it will work for you. Do not question why or by what right you have this power. Developing it is as natural to you as walking or breathing. Like those functions, the power of your protective aura is something that you establish your right to simply and precisely by exercising it. Like those functions, it can help you in many ways if you make good use of it, whereas merely knowing about it will do nothing for you.

Beware of your aura. Other people are aware of it. They feel it as powerful or weak, active or quiescent, bright or dim. The more confidence you have in your aura, the stronger it becomes. The stronger your aura becomes, the more powerful you, too, become.

The aura can be of such strength that even earthly materials and activities may sometimes be deflected by its power. The annals of warfare through the centuries have contained a number of strange but irrefutable accounts of individual soldiers who have stood or advanced unhurt in a volley of missiles, whether arrows, spears, or bullets. Several famed Native American warriors have held a reputation for doing this repeatedly. People in various lands have unaccountably survived through massacres, earthquakes, and disasters of every sort. After the event it is usually impossible to prove the exact circumstances, but widespread human testimony cannot be set aside.

Sometimes people who have been buried in falling buildings, for instance, have spoken afterwards of being certain that if they kept their courage they would live to be rescued, and many other men and women have known that feeling when pulling a car out of a skid, or when jumping across a crevasse, or doing something else that never hit the headlines because it succeeded: "I just knew I could make it," they say. And, "I felt lucky."

It does not explain everything, of course; the many courageous people who have been killed, or the innumerable "premonitions of disaster" that have come to naught and have usually remained inexplicable. But this healthy assurance that helps us make prompt courageous decisions, justifies itself repeatedly as the feeling to live with.

It does not make a person permanently death-proof. (No reasonable person claims that, and a life fully lived makes its own adjustments to that wish anyway.)

- It does mean you live every moment of your life.

- It does mean you live to something nearer your potential—not like a psychic cripple.

- It does mean your powerful aura will keep you from many sources of possible harm.

The harm that does not happen can seldom be seen. A very good example, however, occurred in England in the seventeenth century. So notable was it that it has been commemorated in local tradition to this day as well as being preserved in historical records.

Congleton, in Cheshire, a region toward the border of Wales, was a village so remote that it seemed to be almost in another world from the Great Plague that at that time was killing thousands of people in London. The landowners, farmers, and tradespeople of Congleton heard some news of the epidemic, but little was known about infection in those days and it seems no apprehension was felt when some people in London sent a gift of textile goods to their relatives in Congleton.

Thus the plague came to the village, bringing death to a number of people and blind terror to almost all.

Those who were free to leave, fled. That took away a considerable part of the population, for in Congleton at that time many people worked at home, making the strong metal-tagged leather laces, or "points," with which women's and men's garments alike were fastened. Those who had to remain, or who did not choose to abandon their homes, tried to save themselves by having as little to do with their neighbors as possible. However, this behavior did little or nothing to keep the deadly infection from the fearful, and made matters worse by leaving the stricken untended and dying in their houses.

This kind of thing happened in practically every place where the plague broke out: Congleton was but as the rest, and had neither the organization nor the resources of a large town.

One young woman, however, was not affected by the general panic. She went from house to house, tending the sick, and the plague did not touch her. She rallied the timorous and encouraged the charitable to make a stand against disaster.

In one house, the father and mother and all the children but one had died of plague. Bess—for that was the heroine's name—rescued the little girl from that place of death, and took her into her own home to tend her. Like herself, the child survived unscathed. "Bess of Congleton" is remembered even now as an example, not only of courage and neighborliness, but also of the protection that courage gives to those who go forward without hesitation.

One of the things we can learn from this example is the importance of not damaging our protective aura from within by creating "fear-bogies" in our imagination. More will be said about this in chapter 4; but it is very relevant here to notice how in Bess of Congleton's time and earlier, while other infectious and dangerous diseases such as "the spotted fever" were regarded with comparative equanimity, the mere name of "the plague" had taken such a hold on the popular imagination that it had power to paralyze people's judgment, displace their normal emotions, and sap their resistance.

Such a power, too, in ensuing centuries accrued to the smallpox, when that dreadful scourge was generally called "the Small P." A similar nightmare, again, has cancer threatened to be in our time, and it would be so if we followed the lead of those who name it only as "Big C"; but the saner hygiene of realism and hope is beginning to cut the specter down to size for sufferers and for their families alike.

What, then, should we do, if we find ourselves in a situation in which we are honestly and simply afraid?

It is no use pretending not to be afraid.

Fear is a natural instinct, like the impulses of anger, hunger, thirst, sex, and sleep. Like those other instincts, and like the ability to feel pain, it is primarily a lifesaver. The problem with all these things only begins when they get out of control.

So the first thing to do when you feel afraid is to recognize it (not to necessarily tell anyone else about it).

The second thing to do, if you have not thought it out beforehand, is to decide what, if anything, you should do about it.

There are, roughly, three kinds of fear to be considered:

1. **Rational fear.** You know for a fact you are in a dangerous situation, and you have to consider what measures to take for your safety. These may be planned for an absolute escape (as from a stampeding herd), or for the lesser of two evils (like leaving a sinking ship in rough weather, or leaping from a burning building), or for a calculated risk (as for instance to save another person's life, or to function as a good citizen in time of emergency). Thinking beforehand, knowing your powers, knowing the location of equipment that might concern you and how to use it—these things are not signs of timidity but of practical sense. As a fact, they increase courage by lessening the feeling of personal helplessness.

2. **Habitual fear (irrational).** Almost everyone has some habitual fear that can be called irrational because it is usually out of proportion to the known facts. When we know it is a habit we often can discount it for that very reason, but not always. A "bad head for heights" really does make hazards for a climber, and a young zookeeper who was inwardly nervous of the animals was mauled by one after another of them. After being attacked by the koala bears he was advised to resign. In

any case, it is useful, if possible, to trace the habitual fear to its source.

If, for instance, a person who frequently travels by air is habitually seized with a fear that the aircraft will crash, a statistical study of the probabilities may help, plus an effort to pinpoint any particular crash that may in the past have rooted itself in the imagination, especially the visual imagination. If you can remember nothing in the ordinary way, ask yourself about it last thing at night and see what comes up in your dreams. Beyond that, the attitude should be:

"I know airplanes do occasionally come to grief, but there is no special reason to expect trouble on this trip. I have expected trouble on every previous trip, and have come through intact. If anything should go wrong, I know the drill."

It is no use to tell anyone—even yourself—just to "stop worrying." It is the irrational nature that worries, and you might as well tell a baby to stop yelling, or a cat to stop watching birds. The way to stop any of these things is to distract the attention; in the case we are considering, fix your attention upon breathing steadily and deeply, and progressively relaxing your whole body. (To do these things, an excellent method is "The Creative Plan of Relaxation" given in *Practical Guide to Creative Visualization*).

Relaxation is not all you can do, as we shall explain later. But it is an essential first step. It helps establish your protective aura, which worry only erodes.

The search for the causes of a "habitual fear" can lead almost anywhere. A young woman who lived with her mother gradually found a curious pattern developing: every time they went out together. On reaching the end of the block or thereabouts, her mother would insist on going back to the apartment to make sure the cooker and the lights were switched off, the doors and windows fastened. A few neighbors to whom the daughter mentioned this development were unhelpful, saying such things as, "You cannot do anything about it, it's her age."

Now, the daughter saw no reason why this worry should have anything to do with the age of her mother, who was a very level-headed and realistic kind of person in other ways; and after considering the matter, and watching a little, she realized it was really related directly to the fact that her mother had spent her whole married life—nearly thirty years—in that apartment and in others just like it, and had not for a long time had any new interests in her domestic life. The clue was boredom.

The daughter saw her mother, before going out, go round the place like a robot or a sleepwalker, checking switches and locks. It was no wonder when, after a few minutes in the fresh air and distractions of the street, the poor woman had no recollection of having performed those actions at all! They talked it over, and managed to instill a little more life and interest into the daily routine; but it was still necessary, for a short while, for the mother, with her daughter's help, to be very resolute in not allowing herself to go back to the apartment and double-check. In a week or so, however, all was well, and the habit was broken.

When you know a fear to be groundless, do not toy with it, do not indulge it. Think of other matters. Breathe steadily and relax.

3. **Sudden fear (irrational).** We call this fear "irrational" because we do not consciously know any reasonable cause for it, although if we could see into the subliminal influences that impinge upon our minds the fear might become very rational indeed. Such was the case of the householder that we put forward as an example in chapter 1. His dreams of the old house collapsing, when he had not noticed the physical evidence, could appear as expressing an "irrational" fear.

We have to consider, too, the history of Claude G. Sawyer, who in 1909 took passage from Sydney, Australia, in the *Waratah,* bound for Cape Town.

There were other men who had clear, rational doubts about the *Waratah,* even before that voyage. Their perceptions were backed by knowledge that enabled them to express their thoughts: whether in the precise technical language of a professor of physics, "The epicenter was just above the ship's center of gravity when she was upright . . ." or in plain, seaman-like words, "She's top-heavy."

This latter phrase, repeated, was also overheard by Sawyer in the course of his voyage. He had noted for himself that the ship had a peculiar "slow roll," but apparently the implications of this were not at once clear to his conscious mind, or else he wished as a matter of convenience to disregard them; for on three nights in succession a terrible warning dream presented itself to his awareness.

In this dream he perceived a man in blood-covered armor, raising a threatening sword and calling him by his name. To Sawyer this grim figure must have seemed to represent Death in person, and the message of the dream would not be lost thereby. We know, however, that the dream-consciousness of the psyche has only itself and its symbolism to express whatever meaning it wishes to convey to the conscious mind. No symbol in a dream is wasted; and Death is not usually represented in armor. Still less would a civilian passenger at the beginning of this century have associated armor with the idea of peril at sea.

To a modern interpreter, this figure seems to represent the "friendly shadow" (a supportive function of the psyche) calling the name and showing a sword in warning of danger to the dreamer; while the blood-stained armor alerts the dreamer that if he remains in his present situation, his defenses will not be strong enough to save his life.

Whichever way one interprets it, we are not surprised that after this thrice-recurring dream, Sawyer became acutely aware of the menace of the ship's long roll and jerking recovery. He left when she stopped at Durban, regardless of the laughter of some of his fellow voyagers and of the loss of the rest of his fare. But he was right. Before the *Waratah* reached Cape Town, a sudden and unexpected sea-hurricane sprang up, in which the ill-balanced ship doubtless rolled over too far and was engulfed. Claude G. Sawyer was the only survivor from her last voyage.*

It is evident that by the time the *Waratah* reached Durban, Sawyer's nerves virtually made it impossible for him to remain aboard. Yet the ship had made other voyages safely, in spite of her dangerous defect. Did Sawyer's alerted and highly sensitized unconscious mind also perceive the approach of

---

*The facts of this history are taken from *Darkest Hours*, by Jay Robert Nash (Nelson-Hall 1978).

the freak hurricane? We cannot know, but certainly there are animals that would have been aware of such a thing, and we simply do not know the limits of the possible action of the human instinctual nature.

We can say with confidence, however, that in such a case the means of perception would have to be the extended aura.

In a general way, although for research purposes we could wish we knew more about the life and ideas of Claude G. Sawyer, history gives us a good illustration of the relationship between various functions of the psyche. We can be reasonably sure, from all the circumstances, that Sawyer was not a habitually timorous traveler. Initially, we can see, he had a degree of quite reasonable fear about this voyage. This rational fear, by itself, he probably would have decided to live with. But his unconscious mind took over. If we will not work along with our instincts in time of crisis, they can temporarily blast our obtuse rationality so as to get their way.

We need to cultivate a sensitive ability to listen to all levels of our nature so as to create a true harmony among them.

This is not the work of a day. It may need a re-evaluation of our entire lifestyle. We can, of course, build up what we please around ourselves; the important thing is to reach a point where we do not mistake the habitual everyday clutter for necessities.

Sawyer had to renounce his fear of monetary loss, of time loss, of unconventionality, and of being ridiculed, because the alternative, he was made to see, was death.

To find, and to live by, our real sense of values, will benefit us greatly in two ways:

We shall know what choice to make in any situation of fear in which we may find ourselves.

Our higher self will be more firmly in charge of our life so that we shall have far fewer causes for fear.

But meanwhile—beginning now, at the present time, there is something very practical you can do to protect yourself. Do not forget the long-term work on assuring yourself of your real sense of values. That is important and will save you a lot of worry and doubt in the course of your life. But this method of practical strengthening of the aura promotes courage, confidence, and real psychic protection from the time you begin using it.

We give two forms of it: a "regular" form for leisure use, and an "emergency" form.

A very great deal could be written (as some psychologists are at last beginning to suspect) about the wonders that can be done for you by your higher self, that living, loving, divine flame (he, she, or it as you prefer) that is your being's true center and origin.

As it is a real spark of the divine mind, your higher self is truly divine: it is the love and life of deity in you and for you.

There is the strongest and deepest personal bond between your higher self and you. That glorious being holds the secret, ideal print of what you as a unique individual are designed to be; and your higher self will certainly, with your loving and joyful assent, draw you into fulfillment of that ideal.

That, however, is by no means the limit of the relationship. Your higher self is the fountain, for you, of all the inexhaustible waters of divine blessing. Into that which you imagine for your good or for the good of others, if it but accord with principles of spiritual reality, you can confidently call the light of your higher self to illumine, to strengthen, to preserve, and to bring your imagining to its rightful fruition.

When you read Llewellyn's *Practical Guide to Creative Visualization* (as we have already recommended you should, if only for the Creative Plan of Relaxation there given) you will find many valuable uses for this knowledge. Here our main concern is with defense, but you will find the same great truth in the following two methods to make your aura the luminous and potent shield of spiritual protection you ought to have.

The Tower of Light (Regular Method)

1. Breathe deeply and evenly (keep this up throughout the practice).

2. Progressively relax your whole body. (You could use the Creative Plan of Relaxation, but sometimes a briefer method may suffice).

3. Stand erect without stiffness, arms at sides. (In making practical use of this method, you may not always find it possible or reasonable to stand. If you are walking, walk upright, evenly, calmly, arms swinging loosely at the sides. If you are seated, sit with spine erect, feet parallel and firmly planted, hands palm down on the thighs. In either case, proceed with what follows just as if you were standing. But when doing your customary practice you should always stand, unless prevented by serious health reasons).

4. Visualize all about you a long ellipsoid of intense bright blue light. It extends about nine inches beyond the surface of your body all around, and to about sixteen inches above your head and below floor level at your feet. (Your psychic aura is much more extensive than that, and is usually visualized in silver; but for defense purposes you need it to be blue, and it is easier to create the conditions you need in this smaller compass.)

5. When you can visualize (or simply be aware of) this well-defined field of intense bright blue light entirely surrounding you, visualize within the summit of that aura, slightly above but not touching your head, a globe of brilliant white light.

6. Concentrate your attention on this globe, so that it becomes brighter, glowing white like burning magnesium. (You do not need to look upwards, just sense its presence.) You are making this image to represent the light of your higher self, which is truly there; and you imagine this globe above your head, not touching, because you do not in any way identify your higher self with your conscious self, your ego-personality.

7. Be aware of these two images: the intense bright blue ellipsoid in which you are entirely contained, and the effulgent white globe over your head, occupying the apex of the auric shape.

8. Aware of the brilliant globe over your head, aspire to the highest good you are capable of conceiving; realizing,

though this globe is a visualized symbol, it represents a part of true divine force.

9. When you feel ready, see that dazzling globe sending down glittering white light. This light, filled with silver sparkles, floods your aura and at the same time completely permeates you, coursing vibrantly through you.

10. The outer shell of your aura remains sharply defined as an ellipsoid of intense bright blue, all filled now with the living, vibrant, sparkling, white light.

11. Continue this formulation for some time (as long as you can effectively concentrate upon it) seeing it as a living, moving reality. The brilliance flows down continually into you and around you—it is inexhaustible, for it is a part of the source of all and in your aura it continually circulates, effulgent and sparkling, reinforcing that hard, sharply defined and brilliantly blue outer shell. Be aware of yourself, blissful and alert at the center of this glorious manifestation of divine power. Let the globe fade from your consciousness, knowing at the same time that it has not faded from reality.

It should be evident to you that the more often and the more sincerely you practice this at leisure, when there is nothing to distress or distract you, the more readily and effectively you will be able to perform it at need. If you have difficulty with the visualization itself, you should try at odd moments to visualize some other simpler object, making your mental image of it as sharp and clear as possible. Always remember, any willed visualization is a mental process; you are not trying to produce an optical illusion or an autonomous hallucination, but a symbol that represents something really existing, and that can induce its operation.

There are situations where protection from danger is needed at short notice. In the case of any physical danger, you should of course employ commonsense measures to protect yourself on the material level, but psychic defense can still be an excellent reinforcement when the material defenses have been looked to, besides being a morale-booster for you.

There are also situations, however, in which there is no earthly thing you can usefully do. Such situations can arise if you find yourself seemingly at the mercy of natural forces, and occasionally it happens that one may find oneself in the hands of a fellow-human who might as well be a blind force of nature so far as any appeal to reason or sentiment will avail.

In any such cases, the ensuing Tower of Light emergency method is valuable, although its efficacy is likely to depend largely upon the customary strength of your aura. In other words, do not gamble upon an unearned success with it, although such can occur: you should perform the regular method daily, and (having practiced to a state of proficiency) use the emergency method only in necessity. In such circumstances, it can turn aside or even quell the violent impulse of an assailant, and it can bring a moment's intermission amid the buffetings of the elements. Not least of all, it can calm and illumine your mind, and perhaps bring to your conscious perceptions some all-important details that make a vital difference to your welfare.

The Tower of Light (Emergency Method)

1. Visualize at once the auric ellipsoid of intense bright blue around you, and, within its apex, just above your head, the brilliant white sphere of the light of your higher self.

2. Aware of the brilliant globe over your head, aspire to the highest good you are capable of conceiving; realizing, though this globe is a visualized symbol, it represents a part of true divine force.

3. See that dazzling sphere sending down a glittering white light. This light, filled with silver sparkles, floods your aura and at the same time completely permeates you, coursing vibrantly through you. See the sharp blue outline of your aura's hard protective shell.

4. Keep this visualization for as long as the need lasts or as long as you reasonably can.

When you let the image fade from your consciousness, know the reality of this protection is still invisibly around you.

In situations of purely psychic danger, this method will certainly work for you if you are faithfully and sincerely practicing the regular method. It is an excellent means of "tuning in," contacting your higher self and quickly checking on the perfect wholeness of a strong defense that is already there. In situations of physical danger, too, as we have indicated, especially where defense by material means is impossible, this type of psychic action can have remarkable results.

A middle-aged couple, enlightened and peaceable people, were walking home one night from a neighbor's house where some special occasion had kept them later than usual, when suddenly they found themselves surrounded by a crowd of strange faces: jeering, threatening adolescents who demanded their valuables. In similar instances, the couple knew, handing over money and jewelry had not saved the victim's life.

However, they were both well attuned to the presence of their higher selves. Hand in hand they placed themselves instantly within the tower of light and walked courageously forward. They were no further molested.

It is a pity we have no means of knowing what was the experience of the youthful gang, but we do know this is a typical example of the protection given by the Tower of Light in physical danger.

But can we only employ these methods for self protection? What about our homes, our children, other people we love, and our pets?

We can protect all these. As we have said, the personal aura extends in reality much further than we could conveniently imagine it for our own personal use.

We can, however, by means of visualization and the action of our higher self, make the extensive protection of our aura powerful for all those who are (as people say) "within our sphere."

Babies at birth still share their mother's aura and continue to do so until their own aura is developed sufficiently to function independently. Frequently, even an adult family that lives together will to some extent share a common aura; teachers, too, often notice that a class made up of the most diverse temperaments will nevertheless develop an overall character, a "group aura." In natural life, animals customarily share in the aura of their group or family; domestic animals usually share instead the aura of their human "family," sometimes of one person in particular. All these affinities show us how to proceed.

From ancient times in various human societies, the blessing of a parent, teacher, or elder sibling has been recognized as having a particular value, force, and authority. The elder person can rightfully invoke the light of his or her higher self to protect a younger person for whom he or she is responsible. As our spiritual nature develops, enlarging and strengthening our aura, so the number of people we can encompass within its benevolent power will increase.

For an animal, this act of protection can best be performed by the person to whom the animal is most attached; should the person be a young child, either the mother or the father of the child should do it.

Here are some variants upon the main Tower of Light formula, to show how this can be adapted for special circumstances in conferring a blessing.

For a baby or a small animal, you should stand holding the little one in your arms while you perform the Tower of Light. In visualizing your auric shell, you will "see" this as enclosing both of you. Having completed step eight of the formula (see page 47), give the blessing by saying such words as, "Let the beneficence of the light be shed also upon . . . ." Conclude the formula with steps nine, ten, and eleven.

For an older child, one adult, or a large animal, you can stand or sit; give the recipient of the blessing a hug of real love and remain thus while you perform the Tower of Light (see your aura enclosing both of you). Give the blessing as above.

For one less-familiar adult, you can stand facing that person, holding both hands, arms down by sides, and perform the Tower of Light seeing your aura enclosing you both. Bless as above.

Tower of Light for the Home

If you practice the Tower of Light regularly, the house will share in the powerfully beneficent and protective vibrations thus created. For special efficacy you can, on any occasion while performing step ten of the formula, go through the house retaining awareness of your brilliant aura, place the palms of both your hands upon each of the doors and windows in turn, and utter such words as, "May this door be blessed for our comings and goings, and bar all harm from entering (or suitable words for a window)." Then conclude the formula as normally, with step eleven.

Note: Your aura is not fixed, either in position or in shape. When you stand with your arms at your sides, its shape is ellipsoid; when you walk, it remains roughly ellipsoid too. When you raise your arms clear of your body, your aura will naturally change shape to accommodate them, and each arm remains encased in the auric light.

Whatever shape the aura takes on with your movements, it retains the protective strength of its outline.

· · ·

Checkpoint

- Pinpoint situations in daily life where you feel your psychic defenses could be better. Reflect and resolve upon the changes that will come about for you when your aura is the shining shield it should be.

- Be aware of your aura. Know it will become stronger as you think about it, and as you work on it. Remember: the stronger your aura becomes, the stronger you become.

- If you have a particular fear, recognize it and consider what you should do about it.

- Find, and live by, your real sense of values. Put your higher self in charge of your life.

- Cultivate a sensitive ability to "listen" to all levels of your nature, so as to create a true harmony among them.

- Practice the Tower of Light regular method daily.

- Practice the emergency method sufficiently to have it ready for an emergency.

- See how you can help those around you with the Tower of Light and its variants.

3

Deep Waters in Occultism and Religion

Study Points

1. Stories of occult terrors are usually just that—stories. They are usually based on a lack of accurate perspective of historical facts, or they are outright fiction.

   a. Many times there is nothing "occult" at all involved, but rather superstition, gullibility, and propaganda intended to place blame for an actual event other than where it belongs, or to foment antipathy toward an enemy nation or religion.

b. There are also genuine occult phenomena—such as "psychic vampires": ordinary people who lack vitality and drain healthy people of their energies—usually without conscious intention of doing so.

c. It is also true that a few malcontents, emotionally sick or immature persons have committed acts of vandalism or terrorism clothed in popular misconceptions about occultism to disguise their enjoyment of the resulting shock or notoriety. No occult power or genuine occult practice is involved. Organized occultism presents no cause for fear to people outside of it. Most occultists are too busily involved with their own self-development and with exploration of various modes of existence to be concerned with playing such games.

2. As in any other field, there are charlatans who disguise themselves as occultists to prey upon the weak and gullible—and the best defense is not to be weak and gullible. Again, genuine occultism is not involved, and these charlatans should be avoided.

3. As in any other field, there may be cases where a real occultist (more often a dabbler or rash experimenter), as a result of jealousy or imagined threat, will employ

occult means in a genuine psychic attack on another person, usually another occultist.

    a. In these cases, the Tower of Light fortification of the aura will provide a perfectly adequate defense, provided the attacker is not able to weaken the intended victim's aura from within by manipulating the defender's own imagination.

    b. The common method by which attack from within is attempted is by inducing feelings of guilt.

    c. The best defense is not to take such feeling seriously; and if you do have guilt feelings you can trace to a mistake you have made—forgive yourself.

    d. One of the best psychic "antiseptics" is laughter—and you can always find the humorous side of almost anything.

    e. In addition, the aura's defensive shield can be further reinforced with an individually chosen spiritual sign.

    f. When religious people interfere with your life, your own expression of your spiritual direction will often win their respect and recognition of your right to freedom of belief.

4. Some occult students—especially in their earlier years of inner progress—will be the center of unsought psychic

phenomena: various noises, poltergeist phenomena, isolated instances of ESP, involuntary out-of-body experiences, phantoms, etc.

   a. If the person is a member of a genuine initiate order, the student will have ample guidance in such matters.

   b. All such phenomena result from the uncontrolled release from the student's astral body of energy material—usually in response to the psychic development exercises undertaken, or—in the case of young people—as part of the excess of free-flowing energy that is a natural part of adolescence.

   c. Sometimes groups—such as church congregations—also experience unsought psychic phenomena as the result of released, but undirected, energies.

   d. Occasionally, such release of energy material at the astral level will attract "elementals."

   e. In cases associated with psychic development work, stop the development program and practice the Tower of Light aura fortification three times daily.

   f. In cases where the disturbances may be the result of out-of-balance ritual experiments, an "antidote" ritual can be the best answer.

g. In other cases, giving direction to the excess energies—as in healing prayers for specific people—will bring the unsought phenomena to an end as well as producing a worthwhile program.

5. Keeping a dream diary will often reveal the nature and source of psychic disturbances, whether of actual psychic attacks, or "astral bleeding," etc.

6. Psychic attack is never truly one-sided: the attacker uses something of yours to implant something of his or her own in your psyche—and this interchange opens a two-way channel you can use to "reverse the current."

   a. To prevent attack, keep control over your personal possessions and castoffs from your body: hair, clippings, etc. Also keep information about yourself and your plans to yourself. Give nothing to your enemy.

   b. Never extend hospitality to your suspected attacker, and take nothing from him or her.

   c If you have something from the attacker, get rid of it. Look for small things that may have been "planted" on your person or in your home.

   d. If you have to talk with the suspected attacker, be aware of your shining protective aura as a shield between you and the attacker.

   e. Perform the Tower of Light every night before you go to sleep.

· · ·

Does occultism itself constitute a threat to uninvolved people? Not at all.

If two countries go to war, other people get involved. Bombs can fall on noncombatants; food and other essential supplies may cease to be available to former buyers, and world prices are likely to be affected. The products of much explosion, combustion, and possible nuclear fission rise into our long-suffering atmosphere, and so on. Civil unrest, likewise, tends to spread among the innocent.

Occultism, despite some people's misgivings, is a much more self-contained world than that. Most occultists, like other folk, have little spare time these days, and they are far too busy giving what attention they can to self-development and to the exploration of various modes of existence to be concerned with attacking other people. Besides, dueling magicians, even when such exist, do not devastate country-sides with errant thunderbolts, nor is any innocent person likely to find his or her cutlery twisted up from a psycho-kinesis contest held by unknown persons on the astral plane overnight. Anyone who wakes in the morning to find his or her hair tied in knots, or a leering face scrawled on the ceiling, pretty surely has at least a suspicion of the reason why.

So, what about the stories one hears? What about uninvolved people being kidnapped and ritually murdered? What about the occasional desecration of churches or graves, with strange symbols left thereon? What of the continued (and rather eerie) persistence of such things as the Charles Manson cult? What about killings by vampires?

Here we have a representative assortment of very unpleasant mysteries that have equally varied backgrounds. Many of the older stories turn simply upon conflicting views as to the value of human life. A number come from the Middle Ages, or from more recent feudal settings, in which a feudal lord (such as the fifteenth-century Gilles de Rais for instance) was used to having power of life and death over the people on his lands, whether he employed that power for military purposes, occult purposes, or any other purpose.

Normally, the rights of such a man over his lieges, like the life-and-death rights often held also by parents over their children, were balanced by the equal power held by the religious and secular authorities over the lords and the parents; but where an influential man chose to flout those authorities, his score could only be settled when they ultimately trapped him.

The same situation, of course, applied to an influential woman. There was nothing really "occult" about the deaths of numerous young girls at the hands of the sixteenth-century Countess Bathory, even though she is often referred to as a "vampire." She was simply seeking to renew her youth and beauty by the use of their blood, just as at the present time, with more science but the same intent, a number of women of means avail themselves of the vital juices of unborn lambs. Indeed, many of us nowadays who have a more humane outlook would accord more rights to an animal than Bathory in her time would have supposed a peasant girl to possess.

Historical perspective is needed, too, in examining the story of the valiant but barbarous Vlad Dracula, the original Dracula. The Turks, wave after wave of them, were trying to overrun his mountainous homeland. He defeated them in battle after long and arduous fighting, but had no wish to spend the rest of his days repeating the struggle. So, with feelings of wholehearted rage and revulsion against the invaders, he had his Turkish captives—20,000 of them if the figures can be believed—impaled alive.

That he took enthusiastically to this method of execution and continued it for all manner of offenders, is quite likely true; but certainly, since he meant his reputation to act as a deterrent, he made no secret of it. There was nothing "occult" about it in any sense of the word. The only mysteries about Vlad Dracula were his immense vigor, courage, and resourcefulness, and the superstition of his foes. Even the superstition is very humanly understandable. No warrior willingly accepts defeat by a fellow man, but an antagonist with supernatural powers is another matter.

But do vampires exist? Experience in psychic investigation and rescue forbids a denial. The true vampire is rare. A classic case is that of Arnold Paole, who lived in the early eighteenth century at Meduegna, in a region that is now part of modern Yugoslavia. He attributed his "infection" to a sojourn in Greece, and this is of great interest: stories of vampirism occur in Greek culture earlier than elsewhere, being traceable back to the ancient blood offerings to the dead. Much more frequent are "astral" and "psychic" vampires, mostly human souls whether discarnate or incarnate that, from one or another identifiable cause, either cannot or will not draw their energy from their natural and rightful sources but draw instead on the energy of their fellow humans. In some cases the parasites are elemental beings that have become corrupted by human contacts. Of this latter class of "vampires" more will be said in the next chapter.

With regard to "psychic vampires" of the human and incarnate kind, there is little cause for alarm so long as you know how to deal with them, and so long as you avoid any degree of emotional involvement with them. Consciously or not, they will try to involve you.

They may or may not know what they are doing. Many of them have lost control of their actions, just as a panic-stricken person in the water may not be able to stop trying to seize his rescuer. They vary widely, from the "black" magician who has broken contact with his higher self and so seeks desperately to form a group of students whose energies he can release ritually and absorb, to the poor old dear who always feels better in the company of young folk and has not a clue why the friendliest ones get so sick and exhausted.

You do not have to shun people you suspect may be unconscious "psychic vampires." They may be old people, invalids, and people who seek your counsel. All you need is a technique to protect yourself:

- Do not stand or sit directly facing the person; on meeting his or her gaze, concentrate only on his or her left eye.

- Cross your legs or at least your ankles, fold your arms, and keep them folded if possible across your upper abdomen (solar plexus).

- Speak slightly aside; when not speaking, keep your mouth closed, your head slightly inclined forward.

Going back to the question of "ritual murders" and the vast amount of pseudo-history that has proliferated on this subject through the centuries, an important piece of real history needs to be noted.

In the days of Imperial Rome, a great deal of official tolerance was extended toward religions of various kinds that were not Roman. The imperial government, however, had no intention of applying this tolerance to any religion which was felt to be spiritually separatist or politically subversive; and since the principle of tolerance could not be publicly abandoned, those religions that were considered dangerous had to be declared guilty of abhorrent practices.

A list of such practices was in fact drawn up for the purpose, and included such things as ritual murder and cannibalism, sexual perversions at initiations or at secret ceremonies, and crimes of any kind involving children. Anything to alienate public feeling from the people whose religion was to be condemned was used. Among the religions against which parts of this list was used was the Druid religion (against which the accusation of human sacrifice, although still repeated by historians, only comes down to us from hostile Roman sources) and, of course, Christianity itself.

When under Constantine, Imperial Rome became Christian, the whole system of Roman law was taken over by the Church, including this old list of stock accusations.

Since then, we encounter the list over and over, in whole or in part, but aimed now against those who in various times and places were considered to be enemies of Christian authority.

This has done untold harm in more ways than one. It has bred persecution and massacre from those times to these. It has created unspeakable fears, not only of spiritual harm but also of physical molestation, among neighbors of differing faiths and practices. Even worse, it has given a terrible code and pointed a hideous way for malcontents of every kind, social or religious rebels or outcasts, should they desire it, to act as was expected of them; and from time to time some of the weakest, or emotionally the most sick, have desired to act as was expected of them.

Besides these few extreme cases, there are always more who seek to give an appearance of such behavior, whether from bravado, or for notoriety, or to disguise an act of vandalism, or from an immature desire to see more vulnerable people suffering from shock and horror. Again, there is nothing whatever "occult" about any of this. In a few pathological cases there could be danger, but it would be physical, not psychic danger; if we feel afraid, it's important to identify the level of what we fear. In these nonoccult cases, the appropriate defense is simply the defense against threatened physical violence.

Organized occultism presents no cause for fear to any person who is and who remains altogether outside it and independent of it. There may sometimes be cause to fear the action of nonmaterial forces that are at large in the world, or even of a solitary "sorcerer," usually untrained, who makes trouble in curious ways; and it is one of the main purposes of this book to show the nonoccult man or woman effective methods of self-defense from all such forces; but that is quite a different thing from having anything to fear from organized occultism or occultists.

Above all we would emphasize, if you have a neighbor who burns strange-smelling incenses or who occasionally can be heard chanting strange words, this should cause you no alarm whatever. Such people, whether the system they are using be Eastern or Western, are just very intent on following their own inner course, and in fact they usually take pains to set up an aura of protection and peace around their abode.

The person who is on the inside of occultism is in a very different position. A member of a reputable order, or a pupil of reputable teachers, is well protected by these associates while developing sufficient knowledge and power to protect himself or herself. Knowledge and power, however, are of little avail without personal use and practice, and without personal cultivation of a supportive way of life. In the Llewellyn *Practical Guides* we set out to give not merely the essential means to achieve this or that goal, but also sufficient knowledge to enable an otherwise unaided student or group to build up a good lifestyle for developing the inner faculties.

In general terms, it can be said that the greater your psychic power and your practiced control of it, the more effective your psychic defenses will become. Physical exercise, meditation, psychic work designed for the systematic development of the centers of activity (chakras), everything that will generate psycho-physical energy and habituate you to controlling and directing it, is good. Anything that will help cultivate your self-awareness is good; anything, that helps you see your thinking mind not only as the rightful interpreter and director of your emotional and instinctual nature, but also as the destined vehicle and instrument of the higher self that is the source of all your powers and inspirations, past, present, and yet to come.

There is a time-tested secret known to those who are skilled in the art of living in this material world, a secret that has enabled many men and women to dwell safely in cities or districts reputed to be "dangerous." It consists simply in never being seen in public without evidence of a definite errand, and going purposefully and directly from place to place.

This is not an occult secret , but it can be used occultly. If you take thought to discover what you are about in this incarnate life, if you pursue your true purpose with wholehearted resolution, very little molestation, physical or psychic, will hinder you.

The people who are in most danger in the occult world are the dabblers, the unwary experimenters, and the rash novices who expect all privileges with neither experience nor training to support them. When they meet a "teacher" they do not ask for his credentials—they are only thankful he does not ask them for theirs. They truly learn the hard way (if they live to learn at all); they may have a right to do so, but they have no right to blame occultism for their troubles.

Since, however, even for normally serious-minded students of occultism a little sidetracking in life is almost inevitable, some of the possible results need to be considered.

The likeliest troubles are attacks from other occultists, either through jealousy (reasonable or otherwise), or in revenge, or as a simple demonstration of power. Extremely subtle and unscrupulous attacks are possible and have been known to occur where, for instance, a newcomer to a questionable order had by chance stumbled on an important scheme not meant for the light of day. Such subtle attacks will be considered in other contexts; they are not, however, likely where it is intended only to teach a perhaps overconfident associate a lesson which is meant to bear the "signature" of the giver.

The worst aspect of such lessons, prompted as they usually are by a violent impulse of personal emotion, is that they could really wreck the recipient's nerve; in some circumstances they could shatter his or her courage, confidence, or capacity for occult operation. Against this, however, it must be said that it is the business of a good order member to be "unsinkable," and to maintain a healthy self-image of himself or herself.

In such a situation, the recipient of the attack may well have anticipated trouble of some sort. He or she should have fortified his or her aura by the regular method of the Tower of Light; this is the finest defense, and will be totally adequate in itself, provided the attacker is not able to get inside it through the defender's own imagination. In the next chapter we shall show a number of ways in which this might be attempted; in the case we are now considering, the likeliest manipulation of the defender's imagination is to produce a sense of guilt and of inevitable punishment. This might begin with a succession of suggested feelings not only of guilt but also of fear, depression, and horror.

The very best thing the defender can do, of course, is to refuse to take these feelings seriously; a reaction that is not easy to achieve without considerable practice in "letting go," and that usually is only possible if the defender either knows the feelings to be unjustified or disproportionate, or at least suspects them to have been implanted. Cheerfulness, laughter if possible, is the ideal psychic antiseptic in such circumstances. If another occultist is making a drama over your having punctured his or her ego (for instance), there is no reason on earth why you should see it as an equally big deal.

If there is a matter over which you think a person of power may attack you, and you do feel rather guilty about it, very well. Admit you made a mistake (if you did) and forgive yourself. That is important. Do not brood. Do not let any emotion persuade you there is any magnitude to your blunders. Go out and soak up sunshine, or look at mountains or the sea, or anything that will restore your sense of proportion. Look with love and compassion (and good humor) at your lower self, forgive yourself, and start over. Be ready for life's next adventure.

Your life is like a circle whose center is the divine flame within you. Remember, wherever you may have gotten to, you can draw a straight line from there to the center of your circle and no one can take that from you.

If you make this truly your outlook in life, then you are invincible. Think of Wagner's "Parzifal," who makes one blunder after another, but who, instead of wasting time in despondency, goes on to each new experience as it comes. In the end, he understands everyone else's weaknesses through his own experience, and triumphantly resolves all their perplexities.

Nevertheless, should any lingering qualms remain in the defender's mind, the aura's defensive shield can be further reinforced. This is not objectively necessary, but is meant as a morale booster. For this reason, it has to be done in a way which is exactly right for the individual defender.

This reinforcement consists in adding a visualized sign at the level of the brow, after the aura has been charged with the light of the higher self. The addition of the sign is simply an additional affirmation, It has to be a sign that really means spiritual protection to the user. For some it may be the equal-armed cross, for some the crescent, for others the pentagram, for yet others the Star of David, and so on. Many signs have a long tradition of use as emblems of protection, and are associated with high and powerful archetypal forces in different cultures, but it is vital that each user should choose the one felt to be truly right for him or her, with no outside considerations influencing the decision; only entire self-honesty is good enough for one's psychic armory. The sign chosen should be visualized in brilliant blue light on the brow, and should be maintained in visualization, or at least in awareness, while danger lasts.

However, when it comes to "persecuting" occultists by trying seriously to implant feelings of guilt in their emotional nature, the activities of nonoccult people must surely be noted.

For perhaps each attempt by a fellow occultist, it seems there are at least ninety-nine very competent efforts by people (relatives mostly) who know nothing whatsoever about occult techniques. Fortunately, at the present time, it is recognized that "reprogramming" an adult who is neither criminal nor anorexic is an unjustified disregard of personal liberties.

The real level of the difficulty is psychological. The non-occult members of the family are entitled to defend their traditions and even to commend these to the occultist. The occultist is equally entitled to be politely noncommittal and to go his or her own way. But human emotions rarely keep the situation as simple as that.

On the one hand, there certainly are people who would pressure their families over anything. If their son or daughter had no concern with occultism, there would still be pressures exerted over a girlfriend or boyfriend, over the choice of a job, or even of a hobby. On the other hand, the accusation of exhibiting pressure is quite often brought by the occult-minded against their relatives where no persecution whatever is meant.

There are two main reasons for this. For one thing, the nonoccult members of the family usually represent a standard and an authority that the occultist has been accustomed from birth to respect; and such authority, when represented by people who are in any case loved, can make home life intolerable for a young adult who feels irresistibly impelled to follow his or her inner voice instead.

There is another important factor in this. The root of the occultist's interest in the invisible worlds (or the seer's or the mystic's, for all alike frequently share this problem of family coercion) is most probably a high degree of sensitivity at all levels that might astonish the more conventionally minded relatives. In that case, their most casual wishes can be interpreted by the sensitive as a command, and pressures can be acutely felt that were never meant as such. Love on both sides is the best solvent here.

If, as often happens, the early self-training of the occultist has included practices to stimulate the centers of activity (chakras), this, too, is likely to have increased sensitivity to other people's thoughts and feelings. During a time of family crisis, therefore, it is advisable to stop practices of this kind, and to concentrate instead on simple awareness, visualization, and fortification of the aura. The Tower of Light (regular or emergency method as occasion may require)—that uses none of the centers save that above the crown, is the most suitable and valuable practice for this state of things.

Outside the family circle as within it, the occultist can sometimes suffer violent and destructive criticism from the frightened, the skeptical, and the officious. Probably, we are not far wrong if we suspect all these people are more or less frightened.

The most seemingly hard-boiled skeptic can be the most frightened of critics: after all, just supposing any of the occultist's "far-out beliefs" should hold a grain of truth, what becomes of the skeptic's neat little floor-ceiling-and-four-walls world? It is useful if the occultist can bear this in mind. We are conscious of our own weaknesses, while other people usually do not admit to theirs; but it is a great booster to our morale, and can help us generally to a more mature viewpoint, if we realize the people who act most aggressively toward us are probably doing so to hide some fear or other.

When religious people interfere troublesomely, they can sometimes be brought back to their better feelings of tolerance if they can see you as a person of beliefs really different from theirs, instead of as one of their own who has "gone wrong." People who would feel it was their duty to haul back a strayed lamb, alive or dead, will often respect the liberty of a mountain goat.

An everyday instance of this will do very well, for it follows the same pattern as more weighty examples. Two women became friendly because they worked at neighboring desks in a large office. They did bits of shopping for each other, they shared sandwiches at lunchtime, and they chatted about the news, fashion, and their families. One of the two, Lucy, also had something to say from time to time about the church she attended, the choir, the Sunday-school, and so on. Her neighbor, Madge, never responded with anything similar, but apparently this was not noticed.

One lunch hour, three girls came in from another department, asking around for a wine glass they could borrow. Madge not only located a glass but also quickly found out why they wanted it, and went off to join them in the privacy of the telephone room for an hour of Ouija divination.

No sooner were they all engrossed than the door burst open and Lucy rushed in. Her face was scarlet, and her hair disheveled. Madge could hardly recognize her. In a trembling voice, Lucy delivered a torrent of violent and venomous incoherence against the party, and against Madge in particular, ending with a succession of misquoted biblical references to witchcraft and evildoing.

Much surprised, Madge, however, kept her cool. As soon as Lucy paused, she said firmly, "I respect your beliefs, but mine are different. I respect the Bible, but it is not my rule of life." Lucy quickly recovered control of herself, and left them. Later that day she took pains to "make it up" with Madge (who really had not been offended) and asked if she would one day tell her of her views. Madge had claimed the right to freedom of belief.

When such situations arise, we can often win more respect from people by making it clear, without any expression of disdain or rancor, that our beliefs are different from theirs, than by seeming to play along with them and making a poor job of it.

However, if your beliefs to a considerable extent are the same as theirs, you have a much more delicate problem. Again, fear enters into the matter.

If someone of your own general creed has become irritated or frightened about your occult views or practices, you should be firm but refuse to argue. Never mind about Urim and Thummim, the Witch of Endor, or any other points you could conceivably score. You have to make it clear that you are personally satisfied about what you are doing and quite happy about your eternal welfare. Do not, however, be drawn into any discussion, of the sort where you would be defending your interpretation as the right one (however strongly you may feel it is so). Your friend, evidently for one reason or another, is not quite ready for it. It is "right" for a tree to grow up vigorously, relying for strength upon its own wood and for protection upon its tough bark, but young or fragile trees sometimes need props and fences.

Your friend probably believes his or her prop or fence is the right aid to growth; do not be drawn into that same kind of exclusivism. Make your position clear, close the subject, and, in such a case, keep it closed.

These difficult situations with other occultists, with family and friends, with acquaintances, are not the only ones in which the student of occultism may feel the need of self-defense techniques. (At this point the question probably suggests itself, why does anyone ever become an occultist at all? We can give but one answer: "for love of the invisible splendors.")

One frequent problem is the occurrence (especially during the earlier years of inner progress) of unsought psychic phenomena: mysterious noises, especially at night; the overturning or breakage of objects in the home or elsewhere, perhaps when the student has merely looked at them; remarkable but isolated manifestations of telepathy; involuntary projection of consciousness out of the body, or (by contrast) apparition of the student's likeness to friends or relatives without his or her awareness of the incident; and generally a lot of what nowadays might easily be described as "poltergeist activity." An order member would be guided in dealing with this kind of problem should it be encountered, but the solitary student could easily feel thoroughly alarmed and bewildered.

In fact, the seemingly diverse phenomena we have listed above are all produced by the same cause: an uncontrolled release from the student's astral body of a greater or lesser degree of its energy-material, under the stimulation of the various exercises for psychic development usually commenced at this early stage.

Later, in occult training, when a program of regular activities will absorb or prevent the escape of this energy-material, there should be no such problem; for the beginner, however, its manifestations can be very troublesome.

(As a close parallel, it should be noted how often poltergeist activities among nonoccult people are associated with adolescents or young adults who have much uncontrolled and free-flowing energy, especially those of "psychic" temperament or those suffering from disturbances of an emotional or instinctual nature.)

In such instances, physical exercise, the development of the centers, and the circulation of energy at both the physical and astral level is of great help in keeping the energy under control, just as in the physical body the normal degree of blood pressure helps control bleeding. This loss from the astral body—as opposed to the astral substance extruded but later reabsorbed—is, indeed, called "astral bleeding," and can cause great lassitude besides its other ill effects if it is allowed to remain unchecked.

It is not commonly recognized how often the originator of mysterious "spirit rappings" is the very person who hears them and who may, indeed, be alarmed by them. They occur most often at night, when physical activity is at a low ebb and substance tends naturally to go forth from the astral body.

Sometimes enough astral substance will be given out to form a vehicle for consciousness, and then involuntary conscious projection may take place. When a person prepares for voluntary projection, the extruded astral substance is formed into a replica "body"; but in an involuntary projection this shaping may not occur, and consciousness may undergo the unpleasant experience, which sometimes stays with us as a vividly remembered "nightmare," of drifting in a condition of complete awareness but being unable to move hand or foot, somewhat like being a swathed mummy.

A possible variation on this experience is when a replica body is formed but consciousness does not enter into it, in which case nobody will know of the occurrence unless the phantom happens to be seen by someone who can recognize the likeness. In folklore the creation of such a doppelganger is held to be very unlucky for its maker, although in most such cases the substance returns to its source with no harm done. Or again, consciousness can find itself temporarily transferred to a "workable" vehicle. For a study of out-of-the-body experience, with all necessary directions to develop controlled projection, see Llewellyn's *Practical Guide to Astral Projection*.

The chief danger with astral bleeding—apart from the resulting exhaustion, and the possible annoyance of getting one's possessions smashed in poltergeist activity—is the risk of intervention by elementals.

The craving that some of these beings develop to share in human energies, to the detriment of both parties, will be considered in chapter 4. It is demonstrated in many out-breaks of poltergeist phenomena, where objects are initially moved, and other manifestations occur, in a purposeless and relatively harmless way, but later, perceptibly, another cause of activity comes into play and the phenomena become purposeful and injurious.

At first, it is not always easy to distinguish these activities from those of impersonal forces that the student may unwittingly have aroused by ritual means; or, in a later stage, the activities of a debased elemental could be mistaken for occult attacks by an angry human.

In any case, if you have reason to think you are being troubled by something more than your own escaped energies, *stop at once* any practices you may be performing for the activation of the centers (of whatever type, rousing of the Citadels, Middle Pillar, or other). Cut back periods of solitude to a minimum, including times of meditation. Put off for the present any commencement of new and unfamiliar occult techniques, and give your entire attention, three times daily, to the Tower of Light. (The ideal hours are just after sunrise, just after noon, and just after sunset. Work as closely to these times as you can.)

This enables you, in nautical language, to "batten down the hatches," and to cut off communication with the unseen worlds until you find out what it is that has been troubling you, and can deal with it properly.

To reinforce this condition, make sure you eat well, maintain your spiritual links, but do not forget your sense of humor! Catch up on some nonoccult fiction or a non-occult movie, preferably on television.

If your trouble comes from an impersonal force you have contacted, you are likely to be able to guess what it is. You should recall having performed a ritual of one of the planets, or of one of the elements, which perhaps developed a special zest or which maybe seemed to soar right out of your hands. The remedy in such cases is simply to counter the overwhelming influence by performing a rite, or even a meditation, for the force that is the natural balance to that one. An elementary understanding of the Qabalistic Tree of Life will enable you to identify the force you require.

It is a basic concept of Qabalah that "evil" forces are only good ones that have become out-of-balance and disproportionate; Aristotle in his *Nichomachean Ethics* gives an account of virtues and vices indicating much the same point. Do not make the mistake, however, if you are overwhelmed with Jupiterian euphoria and indolence, of doing a massive rite of Mars to counter it. Begin by "taking your antidote" in mild doses—you can increase them if need be. One meditation may suffice.

Having dealt with the question of impersonal forces and put it out of the picture, how are you to know if you are suffering from any kind of genuine psychic attack? Presumably there will be a sense of there being at some level something amiss, or you would not be wondering about it.

The first thing necessary is to review your physical health. This needs to be done with a perceptive understanding of the interplay of the body with the psyche: particularly with the emotional-instinctual level of the psyche that has so great an effect on our sense of well-being, frequently affecting us just below the threshold of consciousness.

Even Dion Fortune sometimes underestimates that interplay. For instance, in her pioneer book, *Psychic Self-Defense,* she writes, "If the doctor finds . . . some com-plaint such as varicose veins that can obviously have no bearing on the mental condition . . . ." But in fact, varicose veins, untreated, have a very enervating and depressing effect upon the nervous system; and in the early stages when the trouble may be undetected, the sense of malaise and weariness, with the subtle conviction of an alarm being sounded somewhere just beyond awareness, can produce a very definite state of psychic distress.

Similar feelings of depression and alarm can be felt during the incubation phase of an infection such as influenza, particularly in the case of a habitually healthy person unaccustomed to recognizing sickness.

This resemblance between the early stages of incubation of an infection, and the early stages of psychic attack, is informative for us. The same kind of vague malaise, of depression, and of fear or suspicion, can be felt in either case. A bodily sickness, however, will not remain at that phase of development for long; within a week it can be expected to declare itself more distinctly on the material level.

Similarly, a psychic attack must, if it is to function at all, begin at some time to declare its nature on the psychic level.

As soon as you begin to suspect your trouble may be of psychic origin, begin seriously watching your dreams.

Begin keeping a "dream diary," with a record of every dream or fragment of dream you can recall. The way most people find effective is to keep a scribble pad at your bed-side, so that on awaking you can at once jot down anything you recall of your dreams in rough form, perhaps with sketches, enough to enable you to go over the experience in more detail later. Sometimes it helps to carry a small note-book with you, so as to note any further details that may come back to you in the course of the day. The finished product should be the diary itself, written up from these notes, and containing if possible drawings or paintings—not works of art—showing as best you can any feature that impressed you with special vividness in the dream. You can add notes on special associations of ideas if these seem important, but do not attempt interpretations of your dreams. This is rather a different procedure from what is intended in therapy. The therapist wants to help you dis-cover what impulses or images rise naturally from your own unconscious mind: here we are trying to get a clear view of anything that may have been implanted in your unconscious mind.

You may get just what your adversary intends. You may get only a few hints. You may get more than your adversary means you to, and this can be extremely useful in identifying the source of the trouble. Much depends upon your own degree of psychic receptivity, and also upon the patience and skill with which your adversary has observed you (probably by "overlooking" you astrally) and has devised material to fit into your personal idiom of feeling and imagery.

If the imagery or its underlying impulses were too alien to you, of course the attack would fall at once; but the attacker can avoid this if the nature of the attack allows the use of simply archetypal material (that is, feelings and impulses common to all human beings).

To individualize and pinpoint the attack, however, some amount of personal material is usually needed; either (as in traditional sorcery) physical material—hair, nail parings, a worn garment in the possession of the attacker, or psychic material based on an intimate understanding of the victim's weaknesses and deep-rooted idiosyncrasies.

If the attack is caused by a nonhuman agency it must be remembered that elementals, although not intellectually brilliant, and not native to the same bases of instinct and archetypal imagery as we are, have highly acute powers of observation plus a more-than-human talent for mimicry. Also, there are certain techniques by which a human attacker who knows the methods and who is sufficiently malign, can either work by means of an "artificial elemental" or can even dominate a natural elemental so that it will go and obsess the person the attacker indicates. Again, in such a case, the elemental has to be conditioned to the person, just as a bloodhound has to be given the scent of the person to be tracked, or as connoisseurs of radiesthesia like to place inside their pendulum a sample of the substance that is to be investigated.

One implication of this is that psychic attack is never truly one-sided. The attacker uses something of yours to implant in your psyche something of his or hers. If and when this exchange occurs, the chief difference between the attacker's condition and yours is that the attacker seems to be in control of the situation.

Psychic attack, however, takes considerable time, thought, and energy to carry through; and anyone who is so much concerned with you as to expend these valuables in attacking you (whether simply to cause you suffering, or to make you give up a job or a house, or from whatever motive) has already lost some degree of control over the situation, and the attack itself is really an attempt to regain that control. This consideration in itself may boost the morale of the victim. But morale boosting, precious though it is, is not all that is required.

Every psychic transaction that necessitates the opening of a channel between two beings has, or tends to have, its "osmosis": to give in one way is to receive, or at least to have the tendency to receive, in another. Orthodox psychology, for instance, knows the sadist is also at a deep level a masochist, and victims who have perceived this have sometimes "turned the tables."

In the case of psychic attack, such considerations show why the attacker frequently takes the precaution of working through an elemental (or, occasionally, through an unfortunate trance-medium). If the victim, or an adept working on behalf of the victim, simply "reverses the current," it is not necessarily the attacker in person who receives the counterattack.

Any information that can be gleaned from your dreams and otherwise (and in serious cases you should certainly seek a competent helper) may yield very clear indications as to what kind of measures will be needed to free you.

A current can be reversed simply by rejecting it, and turning it back. We shall come to that. Our chief concern here is to prevent the situation from developing.

Strengthen your aura with the Tower of Light, but do not do anything to "close down" your psychic awareness unless and until you feel threatened. The more sensitively you can perceive any possible danger, the more quickly and effectively you can escape from it.

There are, however, some precautions you can take (whether or not you yourself are an occultist) as soon as you know or suspect that a person likely to harbor a grudge against you possesses occult powers. There's no need to show hostility (which is anyway unwise, and you might perhaps be mistaken either about the grudge or about the occult powers); but you can exercise "reserve" in a few inconspicuous yet useful ways.

1. Be even more careful than you normally are about personal items. You would not of course leave hair-combings or a soiled handkerchief about; but equally, do not mislay your pocket-comb or mirror, do not leave snapshots of yourself around, and, if you smoke, do not leave stubs in the ashtray. Should you have to send a letter to the person in question, do not lick either the envelope or the stamp.

2. Do not give information about yourself, either to that person or to any friend who might unsuspectingly be quizzed. This includes information about your birthday. If your associates already know your birthday for celebration purposes, try not to give either the year or your exact age, or at least keep out of any talk that could lead up to your giving the exact hour of your birth. (One

personal-security-minded lady, for years, gave her birthday as being about nine days earlier than the true date—which put her into a different sun-sign! After that the hour or the year of her birth could be given with impunity.) Your horoscope is important personal property. Also avoid saying, for instance, what hairdressers or barbers you visit; change the establishment if need be.

3. Do not let even the most skillful angling induce you to offer hospitality to that person: do not in any circumstances feel you have to offer him or her a drink, a meal or a lift, and above all never invite that person into your home. Supposing that person is occultly not guilty, and you seem to be lacking in the social graces well, too bad, you can't win them all and you can't afford the risk. Supposing that person is really trying to ensnare you, he or she will understand very well what you are about.

4. Having avoided giving anything needlessly of yourself to your antagonist, you should also avoid taking anything from him or her. There is a device sometimes used by sorcerers to disarm and entrap a person of the opposite sex, or by a sorceress to entrap another woman. It is, firstly, to fan an existing antagonism into a real quarrel. It doesn't in the least matter which party is "in the right"; after a suitable interval, the sorcerer apologizes most abjectly, and gives the other person some little token of regret for the occurrence; this may be any small thing, a brooch, a scarf, or even a piece of

candy. But that object will have been charged beforehand, and gives the enemy a foothold. Best not to be drawn into the initial quarrel, tempting though it may be to express some of your feelings; such a situation needs playing as cool as you can keep it.

If you have any object that you have received in these or other suspect circumstances, or anything that seems to "get on your nerves" or to carry some inimical influence, get rid of it. Do not try to rationalize the situation. Burn the thing, if possible; if not, drop it in deep running water. If it needs weighting, attach the weight with nylon or something similarly durable. (If the object is very small, the quickest accessible way of sinking it in running water may be to flush it down the toilet.)

Remember, too, that small objects may be "planted" on you without your knowledge. If you are making a search for such things and you leave your coat hanging in an accessible place, do not forget to lift the lining and look between it and the cloth; also get rid of any unidentifiable keys. (It is well-known that most people will keep those for evermore). In the home, the old favorite hiding places for charged objects are under stairs, carpets, and on the underside of a table or mattress.

Such material objects are nothing in themselves; they can be important because they carry psychic influence that can act when the person you suspect is out of sight and you may therefore be "off guard." One hears sometimes of material objects being charged with great power, objects that because of their intrinsic worth would not be destroyed, like the Hope Diamond or certain Egyptian relics. Most of us are unlikely to be confronted with objects of either such exceeding value or such exceeding power; the great majority of malignly charged objects can either be gotten rid of or, in the case where they hold some value, occultly cleansed.

While you are talking to a person whom you think has occult power and have cause to mistrust, you should be aware of your shining, impenetrable aura like a thick sheet of blue glass between that person and yourself; you should be aware also of your special sign, radiant upon your brow.

When you are away from that person, if you have no feeling of his or her influence still being with you, you can let your aura fade from your awareness but still know it is there. Give your mind to any work you have to do, exercise physically, eat good food, rest; spend time in innocent pleasure, preferably among friends.

Last thing at night before you go to sleep, perform the Tower of Light while lying down, and enjoy a peaceful night's rest.

When you are talking to a person whom you mistrust, you should be aware of your shining, impenetrable aura and your special sign.

Having outlined the kinds of trouble that may center around students of the occult or may be caused by "sorcerers" (people with inborn and undisciplined occult powers), let us glance at some troubles of rather similar types, although generally given less notoriety, that are encountered in and around the world of organized religion.

The reason for the little notoriety is not so much a wish on the part of the religious to "hush up" anything that looks out of place in their accepted scheme of things, as an incomprehension, for the most part, of what may be encountered. Even nowadays for many people in organized religion (and in our context that chiefly means Christianity) there is only God, the Devil, and the myriad human souls that are either incarnate or following certain well-charted paths in the "hereafter." Children may be allowed a guardian angel, some denominations permit a discreet intervention of saints, while the alcoholic, the adulterous, and the irreligious may be considered as victims of the Devil; but there, for the majority of churchgoers, the range of nonmaterial possibilities would probably seem to stop. That is not to say hauntings and other strange happenings are outside their experience or at least outside their hearsay; but these are not given recognition and so have no effect on the accepted pattern.

The religionist differs from the occultist chiefly in relying upon prayer. This should not weaken the religionist's spiritual competence, but it often does.

One source of trouble is that although the faithful have a recognized duty of prayer, a number do not consider they should pray for anything in particular. An enlightened pastor can help by following up such words as "Let us pray for the sick" with a few sentences suggesting visual images of regained health for sufferers, and giving time for the congregation to get round to it. "Let us pray for ourselves," too, should be strong, positive, and certainly not apologetic:

if a church member really wants to do some useful neighbor-loving and talent-improving, he or she should give at least enough reflective thought to self to have a clear idea where improvements can be made or where existing strengths and abilities need maintenance. The relationship of visualization to prayer has some important references in Llewellyn's *Practical Guide to Creative Visualization;* without some such practice one has chiefly the shapeless clouds of blue vapor that C. S. Leadbeater described many years ago as seen clairvoyantly, drifting about in churches.

(It is not our business to tell people how to run their private religious activities; but if you honestly cannot think of anything you really need, then instead of a limp "Lord, you know my wants better than I do," the prayer time could be better spent in thanks or adoration. "We give thee thanks for thy great glory" is probably the finest such prayer ever devised).

For assuredly even the most inert prayer, like any other human activity, even if it fails to produce its proper effect, must produce something. What becomes of that "something" is another question, and the answer gives us the root cause of many of the psychic and emotional problems that people in organized religion often experience: released but unused energy.

Energy is simply energy. Just as the physicist has to recognize this fact, whether a given quantity of energy is manifested in heat, light, sound, or kinesis, so must we all recognize it.

Referencing human activities, we customarily use such terms as "human energy," "spiritual energy," "physical energy," "psychic energy," "sexual energy," and so on, because at the instinctual-emotional level, energy takes on the character of the way it is manifesting or the way it has lately manifested: just as a kettle that has been heated remains hot, or a shout that has been uttered will go on echoing among the hills radiating in sound waves. All these characters taken on by energy are transient, and just as there is no reason why energy coming from a waterfall cannot light a fire, so there is no reason why energy released in "prayer," if it is not an effective offering for its intended purpose, cannot manifest itself in bickering and quarrels, in sexual stimulation, or even in poltergeist phenomena.

The effective nucleus of well-led, energetic congregations in which all ages participate, membership is an inspiration, prayers are fulfilled, and the general tone is one of health and happiness, rarely encounter psychic unpleasantness. Anywhere outside that effective nucleus, trouble of one sort or another can brew up unexpectedly.

The traditional type of church whose members do not really want a religion that "works," who just want to say their prayers and to keep out of sin and to get through this "vale of tears" as unobtrusively as possible, can sometimes develop peculiar hauntings, or curious intensifications and warpings of even the most ordinary emotions; as in a stagnant pool, strange things move beneath the still surface, and the only cure is to open it up, let in light, and movement, and new activity.

At the other end of the scale are the hyperactive, revivalist-type groups where anything can happen and where most things do. It is these groups whose very existence makes the traditionalists thankful "not to be like those," and yet the trouble is apt to be the same in both extremes: undirected energies, whether in massive or small quantities.

What happens when a person with some emotional or other psychological problems comes into such a supercharged atmosphere? Such people tend to gravitate to religion, as also to occultism; but occultism is not bound to accept them.

Again, the root of the trouble lies in the habit so many people have of using the personal-unconscious level of the psyche as a trashcan. All the aspects of ourselves that we do not want, all the things from early childhood we wish we hadn't done, tend to be dumped into it. We can make ourselves forget them. Not only individuals do this: the people of a whole community can build up a tacit understanding, for instance, that they just do not have this or that fault. This often leads, as one very common result, to what the psychiatrists call "projection": the faults people won't own as even possibly theirs, they see as belonging to some other people, and especially to those they feel are most completely "other." Many prejudices gain ground in this way, against one or the other sex, one or another class or race.

The same process of disowning faults can, however, in a very impressionable and emotional person lead to the disowning of a whole area of the psyche that is judged to be undesirable by whatever standard; and when this "splinter" is thus outlawed, divorced entirely from the conscious self, since it still has living energy it can lead a completely irresponsible life of its own, independent of, and even hostile to the normal personality.

Some people whose feelings of guilt (usually fallacious or disproportionate) have led them into a sense of being plagued by "the Devil" have proved to be neither possessed nor simply deluded, but victims of this kind of dissociated "splinter" of their own psyche.

Such a problem is far worse when the sufferer is a member of a small, closely-knit but ineffectual congregation. It is in such a case possible for individuals with some degree of clairvoyance to actually catch a glimpse of the dissociated "splinter" as if it were indeed an independent entity, although an experienced occultist would see what it was. The "splinter" itself can gain increased strength and independence through the unused energies of the congregation. The sufferer will usually try to attend as many services as possible, "feeling so much better" then, because other energies than his or her own are being tapped. A so-called "mass hysteria" situation can easily develop in the absence of clear understanding and firm handling of the splinter being.

Free energy not effectively directed to its proposed end can cause or intensify a great variety of psychic ills among a congregation; but what of the leader of that congregation? Actors and actresses know the heady power that rises from an audience when the performer is "on the beam," the vigor and inspiration that is felt in creative stagework, catching, conditioning, and directing those billows of energy; but theater work is a somewhat different thing from religious leadership, and the same sort of allowances are not made for "artistic temperament" if a pastor gets energy-drunk.

Besides, if a person in that position is emotionally weak or has some undetected psychological hang-up, how many people are going to be affected by it?

If an actor or actress can condition the arising energies to a tragic emotion, so that caught at the appropriate level of response the whole audience is in tears, while concurring with the performer at a deeper level that it's all a play, that is fine acting; but if in predisposing circumstances a devoted congregation is caught up in its pastor's paranoia, then you have a Jonestown.

What, then, should be the standard for spiritual leadership and following, a norm that can be looked for and expected despite differences of creed, practice, or opinion that should be respected? Taking into account, too, that the range of psychological normality is very wide, and that the actions and interactions of human beings are not always predictable?

An important test, as experience shows, is that of maturation: no matter what obedience and discipleship may be expected of the followers in their various stages of instruction and experience, are they allowed the right to mature and grow out of that tutelage? Any normal adult is entitled to this. A religious leader, like a parent, should look forward, in the case of each follower, to the day when that person will not be a pupil but a friend, and will continue to adhere to the movement not through any inner or outer compulsion but from love and from a conviction of its worth.

• • •

Checkpoint

- Watch out for "psychic vampires." Remember, many of them are innocent, sick, or aged people who have no suspicion of how they pull energy out of others; you can help them in other ways if you protect yourself by the method given.

- Continue strengthening your aura by the Tower of Light.

- Do not loiter through life. Put your higher self in charge and follow your main purposes wholeheartedly.

- Do not just dabble with occultism. Come right in and benefit by its protection, or stay in the clear.

- If you have a special sign for protection, practice visualizing it in blue light on your forehead when you feel you need extra aid.

- If you have done anything you feel ashamed or guilty about—look with love, compassion, and good humor at your lower self, forgive yourself, and start over.

- If you think you may be suffering a psychic attack:
    1. Check whether you may be causing your own distress by "astral bleeding" or by some physical malaise.
    2. Watch your dreams. Begin keeping a "dream diary" to discover strange intrusions.
    3. Practice a strict "psychic hygiene."

4. Give nothing to, and take nothing from, a person you suspect is psychically attacking you.

5. Cultivate your protective aura. If you join any organization, whether occult or religious, make sure it will let you "grow up."

4

The Psyche's
Weak Points

Study Points

1. Let reason, not emotion, be your guide. Emotion is fuel to the astral level, and should be used to bring strength to your astral work—but the emotions of fear and desire can weaken your protective aura by stimulating the imagination in the wrong way.

   a. Your well-fortified aura is an invulnerable shield to any attack from outside, but it can only shut out what is outside.

    b. When you form an image in your imagination, this can become a focal point for corresponding forces within your aura.

    c. Learn to get rid of any unwanted images by visualizing some kind of positive action that will destroy them.

2. Sometimes, psychic attack is made through the instrumentality of an elemental—one that may impersonate any other person or being in order to gain your trust and confidence so that, in essence, you "invite" the impersonating elemental across your auric barrier.

    a. Many elementals bask in human emotions, and some have learned to stimulate emotional excesses on the part of susceptible humans—being thus responsible for some types of alcoholism and the horrors of delirium tremens.

    b. People who have been "seduced" by such elementals, hopelessly entrapped because their auras have been breeched from within, can be helped by another person performing the Tower of Light for them.

    c. Satyrs and nymphs are another type of elemental feeding off of sexual energies, prompting acts of hypersexuality, and even rape. (We have a lot to learn about the psychic side of crime and violence.)

    d. Incubi and succubi may not be true ele-
mentals, but "splinter personalities" representing the rejected sexuality of a man or
woman—whether living or deceased.

3. "Doll sorcery" is yet another form of psychic attack—
involving the use of an image made into a likeness of the
intended victim, and then linked to him or her magically so that whatever happens to the image will be experienced in some manner by the victim.

    a. In cases where you can get ahold of the
image, break the link by proper visualization of a cutting action, cleanse the image,
and then burn it—as described in the text.

    b. In cases where you suspect doll sorcery is
being used against you, but you cannot gain
possession of the image, you must still
break the link—as described in the text.

    c. Keep the aura strong and sealed with the
Tower of Light practices.

    d. Practice creative visualization techniques
to fill your imagination with positive
images of things you want. An imagination purposefully occupied will be less
susceptible to breech from within.

• • •

The well-established aura of a person who is physically and psychically healthy (psychic health being the more important of the two) is, of its nature, invulnerable. It is a shining armored defense that can repel any psychic attack and also (because attackers on the material level are motivated by chaotic emotions) can dissuade or even completely dazzle people who might otherwise want to attack you on the material level. Your aura may not, however, protect you adequately if you yourself weaken it from within. Reason, naturally, would never lead you to do this; but emotion might. This is the sort of situation for which students of occultism are trained and warned to rule their emotions: not to turn anyone into a robot, but to help the student stay in control of his or her destiny.

The emotions that might damage your aura can be grouped under two main heads, although in real life they may be mixed together in any proportion:

Desire and fear are two such emotions. While differing altogether from each other (attraction and repulsion—literally "poles apart"), they both operate, or can be operated, in similar ways to cause you to weaken your defenses.

They both tempt you to use your imagination when you should not, or to use it in the wrong way.

Your aura can only shut what is outside. It can't free you from what is inside, or has a foothold inside already. If you form an image in your own imagination, that image can be a focal point for corresponding forces and can introduce them right inside your psyche, bypassing your aura completely. This is true even when nobody is seeking to influence you occultly; when someone is trying to do so, the effect is many times more powerful.

So if you fear something, or if you desire something and wish you didn't, avoid image-making. Admit to yourself you are afraid, admit to yourself you want whatever it is, but do not picture it to yourself; do not above all picture it in action.

Should fear images or desire images begin forming, break them up, scatter them—turn your mind to something different—a hobby, a movie, or an absorbing novel.

Just as it is good to practice visualization so as to form at will whatever images you may choose, so also it is good for defense purposes to practice destroying unwanted images. There are various ways to do this, but the action should be definitive; and as it is generally easier to make a positive action definitive than to do the same with a negative action, it is quite a good idea to link in the positive visu-alization of some image with your act of making the unwanted image vanish.

One person, in order to achieve immediate result, practiced visualizing a brilliant red cancellation cross, becoming instantaneously visible across the whole area of any image that was to be deleted. The image would then disappear, blotted out by the blazing negative sign, and that sign in turn would fade away.

Another person achieved much the same result by visualizing a "grid of darkness" on top of an undesired image. The separated fragments of the image were then visualized as drifting further and further apart, at the same time dwindling, losing clarity and identity.

It does not matter how you do it, but these two examples both show one important feature: the visualizer takes the initiative, treating the unwanted images just as he or she wills.

If you practice doing likewise, this will not only be good psychic training, it will also give you an early warning should anyone try to "plant" an image in your psyche (by suggestion or telepathy, for instance).

You will have become accustomed to the way in which random images vanish, and the speed with which they vanish. Any image that is obstinate, or that in some way does not conform to type, may be considered suspect.

If difficulty arises, however, the important thing is that you do banish the image. In reality, you would be safe if you could learn to disregard it, but where an image has strong associations for you that either attract or repel, indifference is by no means easy. Get rid of that image by visualizing it turning into something else the moment you become aware of it, close down on any form of psychism, and practice the Tower of Light.

In many cases you need do no more. The rejected image will return to its sender, and what happens then will depend largely on the sender's intentions in trying to obsess you (for that is what it is). The intentions of an obsessor are by no means always lethal, and results can vary accordingly; one case known to us gave rise to some amusement afterwards, although it was distressing at the time.

Yvonne, a widow who had always lived in comfortable circumstances, was unwilling to change her lifestyle although she had suffered some serious misfortunes. She had at one time joined a large occult organization but had left this after learning a few of its techniques; and now she secretly resolved to give one of her friends a compulsive idea, "Help Yvonne!" She knew she should not use her knowledge in that way, but the friend, Brenda, came of a rich family and doubtless (Yvonne thought) could assist her just for this time without being inconvenienced.

To everyone's surprise, Brenda suddenly fell sick, with increasing physical lassitude and acute symptoms of anxiety although she had no awareness of anything to be anxious about. Several of her other friends were occultists, and when the doctors were baffled, two of these friends gave her a psychic examination. They found, in fact, an astral "implantation" that they dislodged, and which then drifted across the room in the form of a glassy-looking sphere. One of the occultists made a banishing sign, whereupon the sphere vanished with a metallic "crack"; but, in the moment before it vanished, it turned on its axis and revealed on its other side the likeness of Yvonne.

The friends were troubled, feeling sure Yvonne could never have meant any harm to Brenda. Brenda herself, on being told what had happened, was not only mystified but insisted they should at once make sure Yvonne hadn't been injured by the "rebound" of her astral creation. So they telephoned two others of their circle, not explaining, but requesting them to call upon Yvonne and see she was all right.

The emissaries soon telephoned back, in their turn both puzzled and astonished. Yvonne had seemed to be dazed, somewhat preoccupied, but had told them quite unexpectedly that she meant to go out and find herself a job the next day.

This in itself was excellent news, but showed such a change in Yvonne's attitude to life that the occultists, to find out more, arranged for a meeting of all parties as soon as possible.

Yvonne was horrified when she heard what had happened to Brenda, and at once confessed her part in the occurrence. Then Brenda was upset. "Yvonne, I'd have asked you long ago whether you needed any money, but there's nothing much I can do. I just get a small payment of interest on investments a couple of times a year from the family; I have no access to the capital and otherwise have nothing but my own part-time job. I suppose that's why what you did made me so sick—I'd so willingly have helped you if I could."

Putting these revelations together, the occultists were able to understand also what had befallen Yvonne. Her "Help Yvonne!" message had bounced back to her, affecting her at the same unconscious and instinctual level of the psyche at which she had meant to influence Brenda, and as a result she had felt impelled to go out and (as it transpired) enroll in a training course as an interviewer. Her new career and Brenda's complete recovery were celebrated together.

It is not always so simple, however. You may not at first realize that what you have is an attacker.

It is not easy to detect if an emotion that you experience is being encouraged by some other being. In any case, if the emotion gives you pleasure, you are not likely to think of such a being as an attacker. It must be realized that attackers do not always present themselves in their own person or under their own colors; a human attacker can, as we have said, act through an elemental, while both humans and elementals are capable not only of taking a roundabout way to their purposes, but also on the astral level can impersonate any other being so as to gain acceptance with you. They do not have to know anything about the being they are impersonating: their usual method is to prompt you to do their astral image-building for them, although occasionally they will come up with something you do not know so as to convince you.

The initial objective is simply to gain your confidence so as to bypass your protective aura. Like the evil entities in folktales who can't cross the threshhold of the house without invitation, these beings cannot, in reality, pass the barrier of your aura unless you invite them.

You may invite what you suppose to be a harmless elemental, an angelic being, or the spirit of a person you have loved; but when the barrier is passed, the purpose of an attacker of this sort is to obsess you.

The attacker may be simply an astral vampire, intent upon using you as an energy source; or in less frequent cases it can be a deliberate destroyer. In the latter case, the attacker will eventually allow deviations from the assumed character to appear, but not until the victim is presumed to be too completely in the grip of obsession to be rational. Then, for example, one may find the likeness of a just and kindly father urging the victim to commit a crime (the very possibility which restrained Hamlet from carrying out the ghost's instructions), or the likeness of a refined spouse proposing a lascivious reunion in death.

People have performed the most repulsive and grotesque acts under such "guidance," although in their normal state mere common sense would have prevented them imputing such suggestions to the persons they name.

We must ask, how is it that people can fall victim to such insidious attacks? Why does the shield of the aura not protect? The answer in every case is through a misused imagination.

Extravagant grief over the death of a dear one; refusal to accept separation from a lover; desire to see the death or suffering of an enemy; or the fantasies (sexual or otherwise) of the lonely: any of these can start an unguarded psyche on the production of images, each emotionally charged with energy.

Elementals are never intrinsically "evil." In their natural state they are innocent and beautiful entities; terrible in aspect sometimes (as, for example, the fire elementals of an erupting volcano), but that terribleness is only our human response to the stark power of their element.

If we are content merely to observe them, our interest in elementals can do no harm. There are, however, some humans who find elementals totally fascinating, and there are even more elementals who have developed a craving to absorb human energies and to share in human life as closely as possible. Many elementals who exist at the higher astral levels bask in atmospheres of devotion and of high magick. Some of them linger in places of worship, invisibly urging the devotees to pour forth even more of themselves at that high but still emotional level; some of them are welcomed at ceremonies of power where their stimulating presence helps create the intended ambience.

Human society, however, is not always uplifting, and certain of those elementals that exist in the lower astral levels have been considerably stained by their human contacts.

One sort thus contaminated comprises certain strong elementals that have been designated from past centuries as "demonic," although really no more capable of moral evil than is an animal. During the same times, we find, dogs, pigs, and other creatures were liable to be brought solemnly to trial and condemned for injuries they caused to human beings. These elementals having thus been given a bad name, the sorcerers of past and present have constrained them to fulfill commands, frequently for such requisites as could not be sought from higher beings. Threatened, degraded, familiarized with the most violent and the most furtive of human passions, these spirits and their reclamation have become a major concern for adepts of certain occult orders.

Meanwhile, a great number of lesser elementals of the lower astral world have learned from certain human activities various ways to avail themselves of the energies of mankind. The result, unfortunately, is to turn these innocent elemental participants into the most unpleasant parasites, and to make wrecks of humans; this is seen very plainly in some types of alcoholism and hypersexuality.

Another class of human being with an intensively developed combination of emotion and imagination, although this is generally to a great extent schooled and directed by intellect and will, is the creative artist. Most often, the artist is entirely preoccupied exploring his or her chosen subject-matter, but occasionally a painter will glance at the side-lines, so to speak, to see what can become of unused energies beyond the control of the conscious mind. Some paintings, including masterpieces by Hieronymus Bosch and Salvador Dali, give an uncommonly clear idea of the lower fringes of the astral world.

One kind of parasite is that which plagues alcoholics. Usually, the alcoholic's initial problem is one of the imagination: either the imagined appearance, smell, flavor, and even sound of the liquid itself, or the inviting "golden glow" of a slight intoxication, or images of some situation that prompts escape in drink. If the imagination could be stilled, the urge to drink excessively would disappear.

But, with the elementals participating, this urge will not disappear. When the person is intoxicated, the imagination will more than ever run riot, emotion will respond to the stimulus of the images, energy will correspondingly be released, some of the energy will go to further adding realism to the images, and so on in a spiral. All the elementals desire is to ensure that they have more energy on which to feed, and astral forms in which to clothe themselves. Meantime, inevitably, the victim's physical health as well as general morale deteriorates under the combination of slow poisoning and steady depletion, so the aura is completely broken up—destroyed from within.

When the elementals have sufficient control of the situation, their own distorted images are seen. It has been widely noticed that when people reach the "horrors" stage of alcoholism—delirium tremens—their so-called delusions no longer have the personalized quality of their earlier imaginings. It is no longer the tempting drink, the cruel spouse, or robot society, nor any other pictured bait or goad; now, "things" that come terrifyingly through the walls or the floor may vary in appearance from ant-like to elephant-like, but all are grotesque, menacing, and pain wielding.

These "things" have been seen by other people besides alcoholics. They are depraved elementals that exist in a region of the lower astral visited by a minority of hardy occultists and psychics in the course of their explorations of the universe. A number of such unfortunate entities seduced by, and seducing, erratic humanity—can be seen clairvoyantly, haunting bars and such places where they sense a hope of prey.

Thus, a bar that had a bad name for inebriated clients in the past may close down and the premises be put to other purposes for a number of years. If a new bar is then opened on the site, with a new generation of management and of customers, in some cases the old trouble "unaccountably" starts up again. It is not unaccountable, however, to the occultist who knows the reason, nor to the psychic who sees the waiting elementals, aroused and hungry for human energies.

Needless to say, nobody with a tendency to alcoholism, or a past history of it, should ever visit such a place, no matter what may be its "historical interest."

There is relatively little at the level of psychic self-defense that the alcoholic can do for himself or herself; the first need is to rebuild the personality, and this usually calls for a great deal of caring assistance although, once the victim is removed from any aggravating causes (which is essential) some people have been able to make the further journey alone. Separation from a neurotic or psychotic relative, for instance, is all some persons have needed to be able to say goodbye to their drink problem. It is in all cases, however, necessary to rebuild the personality—perhaps on a more mature pattern than formerly—and to re-establish normal energy; then the aura has a chance to become naturally re-integrated, and practice of the Tower of Light will give valuable help.

In the early stages of return to normality, however, the obsessing elementals will do all they can to reverse or at least to hinder the process; and every means that can be used to help the victim fill the imagination with other healthful images will assist in banishing the attackers and furthering the cure.

Two practices can be of immense value to alcoholics, even in the early stages of seeking improvement. One is their visualization of their special ign. This confers a degree of real protection, and much assists self-respect too.

The other practice is of supreme worth to one who in those early stages cannot effectively perform the regular Tower of Light. A friend should frequently perform for, and with, the sufferer, one of the "variant" techniques given on pages 51–52.

Hypersexuality is another human condition in which elementals have become considerably involved, and which very often is either caused or greatly increased by them.

Ordinary sexual intercourse between regular partners is not greatly troubled by elementals; the two persons concerned are accustomed to exchanging their energies, there is no high level of emotion, and there is nothing to impair their auras—or we may say in such a case, their joint aura. Where there is any feeling of guilt, which is basically a form of fear, the aura is likely to be weakened; and intercourse where there is an emotional and therefore energetic reaction of unusual violence (which sometimes accompanies a "guilt" situation) is liable to attract elementals.

The hypersexual woman is often termed a "nymphomaniac," from the old-time belief that she was obsessed by the nymphs, that is by nature-spirits, elementals; and, although the initial cause of her trouble might be physical or, probably, psychological, the ancients saw truly that she was soon surrounded by a throng of elementals invited by her febrile imaginings, feeding upon the emanations of her energy, and without fail, presenting ample material for further imaginings.

The word "nymph" means bride, and has been given from ancient times to gentle beings that have an affinity with female nature. Drawn to a female personality, they try to make the human more and more like themselves.

Two things, however, the elementals cannot do. They cannot comprehend the existence of human standards of sexual morality, for in their native world the free give-and-take of energy in any manner is simply a natural enjoyment, and has none of the connotations that sex has for humans. Consequently, they cannot comprehend, and so can never really learn, that there exist many human beings who are content to accept the dictates of society and are not at all eager for opportunities to break loose, but find security in their solidarity. The elementals are quite unable to perceive the problems they create for their human victim, destined to live in a society from which the nymphs have alienated her.

There are other elementals that possess, or have acquired, an affinity with male nature. These satyr-entities, when they attach themselves to a man, proceed to make him as much like themselves as possible. They enhance the imaginings that first formed a bond between him and them, they prompt acts of sexuality and rape of which, again, they can in no way comprehend the human implications of; nor can they understand those complexities of human nature that makes of something they themselves see as a joyous and spontaneous sharing of life, so often a matter of tragedy and destruction for the human participants.

The two types of entities just described remain "behind the scenes" in their activities. Others exist, however, which manifest themselves almost physically.

These are the entities that have been named in the past incubus or succubus. They would seem generally to be of human origin: rarely an entire "earthbound soul," sometimes the consciousness and astral vehicle of a living person, but often a psychic fragment—one of the "splinters" previously mentioned—representing the repressed and rejected sexuality of a man or woman whether living or deceased. (In the latter case, there is the possible complication that this "shell" may be taken over and given, as it were, a new lease of "life" by an elemental of like inclinations).

These entities are comparatively uncommon—or at least are comparatively rarely known of—but they are of unmistakable reality, existing at the very low astral or "etheric" level, just beyond the material world. To manifest themselves, they draw the necessary extra amount of astral substance freshly from their partner at the time, and so can be considered vampiric just as, or even more specifically than, the ordinary sex elementals. (They are also much more jealous and possessive).

They appear as human beings, with bodies firm but abnormally supple, boneless, and very smooth. We may call to mind that the true manifestations of ectoplasmic bodies, such as occur at physical-mediumship séances, have sometimes been fraudulently mimicked by the use of latex gloves filled with water and sealed; this gives an idea of the texture of the genuine article. These entities are similar, save that they lack the clammy chill.

This description is based upon cases that were known to us many years before the beginnings of life-size inflatable dolls; a very curious example of the way we frequently see earthly inventions follow upon astral patterns.

The entities themselves, however, behave very much as living beings. While a student, one young man had for some years received the attentions of a "lady" of that kind without finding anything undesirable in the association. Then he got married, assuming apparently that his entity-friend would easily take the hint; but he learned differently.

The first thing he knew of the true state of affairs was a cry from his bride, "Move your arm—it's across my throat!" followed by a horrified "There's someone else in the bed!" The jealous entity had in fact materialized between the two embracing humans, and the husband had no choice but to ask his wife to go into another room while he pacified and dismissed the intruder. After several such occurrences, he had to seek occult help, or his marriage would have ended. The entity proved to be an elemental that had taken over the "astral shell" of a nymphomaniac who had died a violent death, so that it was still imbued with her unruly instincts.

A man and a woman who are sexual partners will normally absorb a considerable amount of each other's energies, especially in their early days together; because she is naturally lacking in male energy, he in female energy. With the psychologically maturing give-and-take at other levels also, this mutual absorption, over years of marriage, helps to effect a balanced development and so tends to produce an inner integration in each partner. Thus, relatively little of the energy that is released by their union remains unabsorbed, unless they deliberately take measures—as in tantra—to keep this energy at a high level; in which case there is an explicit purpose for the extra energy, so it still does not remain unused.

Solitary people who masturbate frequently, with accompanying morbid, violent, or degrading fantasies, occasionally become victims of elementals and/or of astral vampires and voyeurs, any of whom will build up a further whirlpool of chaotic fantasy around them and draw them deeper into unreality; mostly preying on their energy, too, as there is no partner to help absorb this. In the modern trend toward broader and more natural attitudes in sexual matters, a great deal of honest puzzlement has developed about the old-fashioned taboo on masturbation. Indeed, masturbation is natural and healthy; the modern attitude is right for the vast majority of people, and hardly anyone need worry about it any further. (Fantasizing is natural, and fine too.)

At the same time, the idea so popular with the parents and guardians of past generations, that this practice could possibly cause nervous disorders and even insanity, were perhaps based on a few people's knowledge and experience even if that knowledge and experience was misinterpreted for lack of the occult facts.

Humanity has come up with various answers. Its most sweeping and yet least practical one is simply to avoid sex. To avoid sex is not, however, as easy as it looks (even if you think it looks easy). In the present context it would have to mean not only avoiding acts of sex and avoiding thoughts, emotions, and instinctual impulses of sex, but also avoiding repressing these into the unconscious. This requires either higher spirituality or waiting until you reach a very, very advanced age.

So, what is to be done by way of self-protection against unpleasant or dangerous entities that can turn natural enjoyments of sex into a nightmare of slavery and sickness?

The more reasonable attitude is to accept the instinct as part of your life, whether you are going to respond to it completely or not. Admit to yourself frankly that you enjoy the company of people who attract you physically. Enjoy your fantasies, but keep them wholesome and in accord with enlightened human values. Sex and self-respect make a great team.

If you really feel you are oversexed for comfort in your present circumstances, there's an easy, harmless way to deal with that (unless you are allergic to carrots.) This has long been known to the occult orders, and works equally well for men and women: just a wine glass of raw carrot juice first thing every morning for about three weeks.

For actual psychic protection there are three main methods: the Way of Prayer, the Way of Meditation, and the Magical Way. A sound, healthy aura is a basic prerequisite for each of them; beyond that, what is needed is for you to establish a way to prevent yourself damaging your aura from within and, should this occur, to deter astral predators. For a sound aura, practice the regular method of the Tower of Light and avoid guilt situations.

If you are doing something you feel guilty about, you need either to stop doing it or to stop feeling guilty about it. We cannot decide for you which it should be, because we do not know the position. If you can 't stop doing whatever it is and also can not stop feeling guilty about it—then you need counsel.

If you choose the Way of Prayer, you probably already have your favorite prayers. If you haven't, and want something traditional, either the Eastern or Western form of the Office of Compline is strong and powerful. Conclude with the Tower of Light.

For the Way of Meditation, again, keep to your favorite methods but, at the conclusion, visualize your aura shining complete and whole about you with all of your physical and psychic energies gathered within it; then proceed to the Tower of Light.

The Magical Way is differently based. The magical principle concerning sex energies is not to limit their effusion, but to contain them and (like the waterfall energy that can heat a house) to give them a new direction and purpose. There is much more to be said on this subject than can be given brief treatment in this book; the implications and conclusions that can be, and have been drawn from this simple statement for practical use in both Oriental and Western traditions, have for centuries attracted deep study and research.

A different form of attack on the integrity of the psyche, one that has been included among the arts of sorcerer and sorceress in numberless times and places, can be given the general name of "doll sorcery."

The object employed can vary from a mandrake root—or even a "poor, forked radish with head fantastically carved"—to a wooden or waxen image skillfully shaped to the exact likeness of the intended victim, and dressed in carefully copied clothes. The impulse is almost universal. To make an image representing an enemy, or a person loved or desired; to treat that image as one would wish to treat the living being: these things seem built into the human race. The caveman sent a dart, or a line of black pigment, to the heart of his pictured bison; people kiss photographs of a child or sweetheart, the devotee places flowers before a representation of God or saint. Each person is seeking to create a link with the reality represented. That explains why doll sorcery is so widespread, and also why it is so feared.

Real doll sorcery is in fact a true magical operation, although at a low level. Even specialists in occult knowledge sometimes make mistakes about it; for instance, we read that it only succeeds because the doll forms a focal point for the sorcerer's powers of concentration, and hence it is the sorcerer's mind, willing a certain outcome that really controls the operation throughout.

That last statement is only initially true. The work of making the doll look as realistically like the victim as possible (where, indeed, this is done) is of use chiefly to help the sorcerer's mind identify doll and victim; but the "magical link" created by whatever means between doll and victim is the truly operative part of the procedure. Once that is established, not only can the sorcerer use it to induce this or that condition in the victim, but also whatever befalls the doll will be experienced in some manner by the victim, whether the sorcerer intends it or not, whether the sorcerer knows of it or not.

This state of affairs is most important to remember should you manage to get possession of a doll that you suspect has been magically linked to yourself or to some other person.

The first thing you must do with such a doll, is a "Breaking of the Link." Look at its outlines in a rather dim light. You may never have tried any form of clairvoyance before, but it's quite likely you may just be able to see a sort of faintly luminous cord reaching out from the surface of the doll and either leading to yourself or fading at its far end into the air.

If you do not see it, never mind. You can do magick, too. So visualize such a cord, leading from the "solar plexus" region of the doll and going off into the air.

Now take a knife: either a solid knife you have with you, or a visualized knife: in either case, please, a clean, sharp, bright blade. See it as flame. And with it, using one strong decisive stroke, you sever the cord at a point near the doll.

You may have visualized the cord, you may have visualized the knife, and you may lack experience of what comes next. But if you have performed the severing properly and effectively, you will know it. The ends of the cord will fly apart, twisting away from each other, seared as well as cut so there is no possibility of their rejoining. You'll "feel" it even if you do not "see" it.

If you do not get this decisive reaction, repeat the procedure. If the sorcerer is an "old hand" and you are not, you may have quite a struggle to sever the cord.

But you can and will succeed.

When once this essential severance is performed, you can proceed although there may still be minor links. Carefully remove any clothing from the doll, taking special heed not to lose any fragments of fabric, locks of hair, or anything else that may have been taken from the victim. If there are any stuck-in pins and they come out easily, take them out; if they are in firmly, or if nails are hammered into a wooden image, leave them.

Now you need a good quantity of water: running water if possible, like a stream, or a bath or a kitchen sink with the water running and the plug out. A wooden or a waxen image should be scrubbed; an image of soft fabric should be washed and then taken apart under water. (You may find more bits of fabric, or other things belonging to the victim, inside). While washing the image, repeat, "This is mere wood" (or wax or cloth).

After this, gather together all the garments and any identification objects you have been able to find, visualize a cord leading from the pile, and perform another Breaking of the Link ritual just as described above. Then, thoroughly burn to ashes everything in that pile (first drying them if necessary, of course). Scatter the ashes in running water, or the ocean.

Finally, burn the image to ashes. Scatter these, too, (with any burnt nails, or whatever, which may have been embedded) in running water or in the ocean. That concludes the matter.

To Protect Yourself Against Doll Sorcery:

1. If you feel some person is already using doll sorcery against you, or some related method to feed ideas into your mind, you probably will not be able to get hold of the doll, so perform the Breaking the Link ceremony upon yourself. It's just as effective. First, perform the Tower of Light to seal your aura. Then, take a new knife, washed and dried, which you will afterward put away and keep from other use; or visualize such a knife. Proceed as on pages 118–119. Unless you have a strong psychic sense of there being some other point of attachment to you, picture the cord as attached in the

region of your solar plexus, and sever it about eighteen inches from your body (do not cut yourself). When the link has been broken, take a bath and put on entirely fresh clothes.

2. As a general precaution, keep the aura strong. Practice the Tower of Light regularly.

3. Resist unwanted fantasies. They can be a first indication of interference, and if you can stop the trouble at this stage there will be no need to take other measures. If you do not want a certain person in your life, do not entertain even from curiosity any thoughts of love or sex with that person. Similarly, if you keep getting a notion that there's something wrong with your health, and your judgment disagrees with it, dismiss it. If it comes back, get a proper medical checkup. Do extra exercise, or study holism: cultivate health-mindedness instead of sickness-mindedness.

4. Take up, or intensify, creative visualization. There must be a few things you want in life—and no other person will stand much chance of filling your imagination with their images, if it is already occupied with your own creations.

5. Choose your own friends, and spend plenty of your spare time in their company. Be interested in their hobbies, and other activities.

6. Do not leave "bits of yourself" around. With regard to doll sorcery, another useful point is not to make known all your names, because dolls are sometimes "baptized" for a person. Many people have a confirmation name, or some other, which they never sign. Keep it that way, but, privately, remind yourself sometimes that the unused name is part of the appellation that means "you."

• • •

Checkpoint

- Everyone has desires and fears. You can keep yours from weakening your aura from within if you keep your image-making faculty under control.

- Do not picture what you fear; especially do not picture it as active.

- If you think something you desire could be dangerous for you—do not picture it.

- A hobby, a movie, or an absorbing novel are excellent ways of getting your imagination otherwise occupied.

- Have a technique like the ones described in this chapter, to change or destroy unwanted images.

- Learn the Breaking the Link procedure given in this chapter in case you need it sometime—it has many uses!

- Keep up your Tower of Light practices.

5

Meeting Impersonal Aggression

Study Points

1. Factors of noise, crowding, the demands of modern urban and business life, and other impersonal forces can "tear at" the aura, and bring about conditions of fatigue, lowered resistance, and even illness.

    a. Some of the noise factors can be reduced at their source, and others insulated against. Some require a decisive act against the accepted norm. Some forms of rock music, for example, are "wrong" for the human psyche.

b. To restore yourself in a stressful environment, perform the Tower of Light at the start and finish of each day.

c. During the day, when you can arrange it, and especially before an anticipated stressful situation, take ten to fifteen minutes for a cycle of relaxation, aura fortification, and attunement with the higher self as described in the text.

d. In addition to such attunement, it is vitally important to take a moment now and then to turn within and reflect upon the lower levels of your psyche: your goal is wholeness.

2. Develop your personality. Be true to your own self; your lifestyle can be a meaningful expression of a life of continued growth and development. Learn to base your decisions on real facts, not on what other people think you should do or be.

a. Learn to express your own real tastes and interests; develop activities beyond the demands of job and family to reflect your own individuality.

b. Keep your personal unconscious free of repressed material—both personal and social, i.e., do not become a vehicle for the prejudices of church or community, acting on standards that are not your own.

    c. Learn to be self-sufficient at least in some areas of life, or gain the know-how so that you could be self-sufficient. (Survival courses need not mean paramilitary exercises, or belief that civilization is about to collapse.)

    d. A "craft" can be both a form of self-sufficiency and a means to the development of your own tastes and interests. "Working with one's hands" is an integrating experience for mind, body, and soul.

3. Anyone interested in psychic and spiritual progress should give consideration to a vegetarian diet.

    a. As discussed in the text, a vegetarian diet can become part of a consistent personal lifestyle resistant to factors that can induce stress.

4. Psychic rapport with the forces of life can be attained through a self-controlled and purposeful lifestyle—and this rapport can give a person psychic influence over rodents and small creatures in the environment.

. . .

Even when no person or being has any specific will to attack us, we can still suffer a certain amount of damage or danger from our environment.

So many factors in daily life, especially for the city-dweller, seem to be arrayed like restless fingers plucking and tearing at his or her aura, or, worse, plucking and tearing at his or her central consciousness and sense of identity. Unrelieved stress, the sometimes fictitious urgency of daily tasks, the necessity of living against a background of irrelevant and purposeless noise, all this can weaken self-awareness and inner identity. Physical symptoms such as headaches and neuralgia, whose natural effect would be to take the sufferer out of those chaotic surroundings for a breathing space, are frequently just given the quick slap down of a painkiller, whether in tablet or alcoholic form.

It is useless to try to "fight" the situation in this way, for the result is still more stress and, by the emotional and physical effort this involves, you are depleting your own vitality even further. A usual result, and one that afflicts many people in different walks of life, is an almost perpetual tiredness.

Before going on to the psychic self-defense aspect of the matter, you might first consider whether you may not really need more sleep. Many of our parents and grandparents assumed an adult needed only to go to bed at midnight to be able to start bright and early on another full day's work; but noise, stress, and city crowding have grown considerably in these last years. There's an even older tradition which says each hour's sleep before midnight is worth two after that time, and perhaps more of us should give heed to it now. To refresh the whole body, including the nervous system and the brain, there is absolutely no substitute for sleep.

But you can defend yourself against continual mindless assault. True, you get nowhere by resenting it, hating it, or by thinking how bad it is for you.

It didn't get to be the way it is by considering you, and you will not defend yourself by thinking about it.

We shall deal with human demands in chapter 6. You can put into practice and strengthen yourself, first, by working on the impersonal "attacking forces."

If you are aware of impersonal pressures in your working life, there may be practical angles you should be aware of. Is external noise excluded as well as it should be? In an open-plan office, are there flock-surface screens or other devices to baffle sound coming from machines in other sections? Is the temperature right for work, and is ventilation or air-conditioning adequate? Do not talk at large about your problems, but take a look around to see if other people suffer from the same things. If others, too, are drowsy every afternoon, or if everyone seems unduly accident-prone, you might come up with something useful. (Management or welfare aren't necessarily hostile, they just weren't appointed for their telepathic abilities.)

Music is sometimes an unsuspected cause of trouble. Taped music, including "classical," is mostly a helpful accompaniment to all types of work; but a few kinds of music, notably some kinds of rock, have rhythms or cadences that are just "wrong" for human structures. They distract, cause fatigue, make optimum effort impossible, and can promote accidents.

Apart from taking a practical interest, however, and there may be nothing you usefully can do to change conditions in your working environment—the method you should adopt for self-defense is to separate yourself from the outward scene during one or more definite but brief periods every day.

Begin and end each day with the regular method of the Tower of Light, not forgetting also to find time for preliminary relaxation whenever you can. And during the day, once or twice but especially before difficult interviews or other situations you anticipate will be stressful, perform the following:

1. Be seated anywhere you can be sure of avoiding interruption. This may be at your desk during your lunchhour, or elsewhere: a restaurant table is possible, with a cup of coffee before you. You will want ten or fifteen minutes for this practice (twenty should be the outside limit) but you will not want to keep looking at your watch, so until you are used to it, if you do not have an alarm watch, either try to start ten or fifteen minutes before some external signal, or get a friend to call you, perhaps by telephone.

2. Relax progressively, from toes to facial muscles.

3. Perform the Tower of Light regular method, as far as Step 9, visualizing light descending from the shining

globe above your head, flooding your aura with its radiance (this time however, without the silver sparkles), permeating you, coursing through you.

4. Now breathe deeply, gently, steadily, in and out: with every "in" breath, feel you are drawing the vibrant light more thoroughly and effulgently into every fiber and recess of your physical body, brain, and nervous system to help you control your life, to help you realize your hidden potential, to help you live with and by, powers and abilities you may not know you have. With every "out" breath, see the vibrant light becoming ever more radiant. It enfolds you, encompasses you in its protective beneficence guiding you in your actions, counseling you in your doubts, strengthening you in resolution and endurance, loving you in every moment, supporting you in every inner and outer impulse of your life.

5. After this, see the auric shell becoming a richer, deeper blue, and the coursing light as becoming suffused with golden sparkles.

6. Then let the formulation fade from consciousness, knowing it has not faded from reality.

The fact that your higher self can intervene, if you are willing, to help you in situations your rational mind can't cope with, is a truth that is being more and more recognized even by psychologists trained in the old school of medical materialism. The rational mind, for so long considered supreme in the psyche, has increasingly puzzled the experts by its limitations. Now experts are beginning to realize it is not, after all, the psyche's ultimate arbiter. The rational mind is like an able eleven-year-old who, in the absence of parents or teachers, can take charge of the toddlers fairly adequately; decisions will be made and the essentials will more or less be kept going. But, at last, the experience and foresight of an adult is needed, to take charge both of the emotional infants and of their rationalistic young guardian.

Barbara Brown, in her book *Supermind: The Ultimate Energy** makes an important contribution consistent with this viewpoint. Her loyalty to the traditional medical viewpoint, that "mind," including "supermind," is an emanation from the brain, is a good thing insofar as it will probably lead to her valuable work receiving recognition from authorities who might otherwise reject it; but she and they have yet to reckon with the plain philosophic consideration: how can the brain originate something that is superior in action and of greater vitality than itself?

We do not expect the doctors and the scientific researchers to accept at once the truth that is known to every mystic and every Qabalist: that the higher self, or "spirit" of the individual is the senior partner and origin of the whole lower personality: body, brain, instincts, emotions, and rational mind alike. Just as they would consider this nonproven, however, so their own, contrary, assumption should be recognized as not only nonproven but incapable of proof.

---

*Published by Harper & Row, New York (1980).

Their work—their worthy and increasingly excellent work—is not to theorize but to give facts to us all. Basic facts are, that the brain exists, that the body with its various nervous and glandular laboratories exists, that instinct, emotion, and logical thinking are closely tied up with these. And there is this other phenomenon: "spirit," "supermind," "the higher self." We do not strictly have to know how it got there, but we do need to recognize its existence and to give it its rightful place in our lives.

While it is important for you (especially during times of stress, and in worry situations that your rational mind has customarily struggled with alone) to make the special effort of communing with your higher self by the method given above, those occasions should not be the only times you recognize its presence.

Make a habit of closing your eyes for a moment now and then, giving just a "glance" inward, no words, just silent love and trust.

It is also essential that besides this building up of the strength of your psyche at the highest level, "getting back to source," you should also maintain—or if necessary restore—its integrity at the lower levels. The vital importance of this integrity to you in psychic self-defense will be made very clear in the next chapter, even if you do not see it yet.

You do not have to be a perfectionist (perfectionism is really a defect in itself) but you do have to be clear about what matters to you most at present, and why you do things. Sometimes you deliberately have to choose to do something that matters more to you, thus rejecting something that still matters, but matters less. And what matters more to you may be to give pleasure to some special person.

That's fine. It pleases you to please him or her, and it's still your choice.

What is self-destructive is when a person dresses, or eats, or expresses opinions to please a crowd of people who really do not care what anyone wears or eats or thinks, so long as the person does not dither about it. Most people like to appear important. Most people fear a rebuff. This means, if you dither about your habits or your views, everyone will delight in "putting you right" according to their ideas, because then they assume a position of importance. But if you behave and speak firmly and decisively, most likely they'll just accept you as you are without giving the matter another thought. In any case they are not likely to speak to you about it —you might rebuff them!

Of course, people can't always do as they please. If, for instance, you are a man working in a place where men have to wear ties, and if your job suits you or you are hoping for a promotion, you won't stick your neck out without a tie on it. But then you know what you are doing and why, which is a very different thing from just acting scared.

In any case, whoever you are, you should make sure your spare time and your vacations are spent in activities that express your real tastes and interests. If this is not so, your lifestyle needs changing fast.

It is a fact that there are many adults who, outside their working hours, exist only as part of a family unit. As it is only the young child who is contained within the parent's protective aura, the adult of undeveloped individuality is in a particularly vulnerable psychic condition.

How is anyone—says a young adult—to begin developing his or her personality? The first thing needed is information, a lot of it. On every area of life in which there are decisions to make, a person should get as much real information as possible.

This involves a fair amount of decision making, but not so much as might at first appear. Major decisions, when made, usually carry a number of lesser decisions along with them. (If you join the army you do not have to decide what color clothes to wear.)

The concern of the Llewellyn *Practical Guides* is with people who believe the development of their inner faculties, and an approach to the realization of their potential as human beings and as individuals should be a primary concern in their lives. Thus in the present book, while our main purpose is to show you how to act so as to guard yourself psychically from various kinds of attack, it is also our concern to give you pointers toward a physically and psychically healthy life, which will naturally strengthen your powers at all levels and will prevent your attracting attack.

Diet has always been recognized as an important part of a person's lifestyle, linking the individual with certain traditions and certain codes of belief or behavior. Brahmins, Buddhists, Christians of various denominations, Jews, Muslims, and people of other religions all have their distinguishing dietary customs. We of the Western occult tradition can truly say that for us in the matter of food all things are lawful: we do not accept any traditional restrictions for the mere sake of tradition. At the same time, each person has his or her own bodily constitution, temperament, and emotional nature; and some people, of their own free choice and as a personal matter, have made a pact with a deity or with their own conscience. All these limitations are involved in the question of our bodily, psychic, and spiritual health.

The relationship between vegetarianism (or more accurately nonmeat diet, since most vegetarians admit milk and milk products, honey, and frequently eggs to their food selection) and psychic self-defense needs to be examined here. We do, frankly, recommend vegetarianism very strongly to students of occultism and aspirants to inner development, for several reasons. Economic considerations are frequently important to young people who want much of their income for other things than food, but who value their health: good meat is expensive, and inferior meat products ought never to be eaten at all. Esthetic considerations, too, can be of great importance to the sensitive, who can be dangerously put off preparing adequate meals for themselves if the early stages are too unattractive. There is also the question of health, and in fact many people are vegetarians for health reasons, to whom none of the other considerations are of any importance. Questions of conscience, however, and conscience on several different points—undoubtedly outweigh all those other considerations in forming people's decisions to adopt a vegetarian diet.

There is the first humanitarian consideration, an unwillingness to prey upon our sentient fellow-beings while we live in circumstances that make this altogether unnecessary. A second consideration (second, because the first one was recognized by many civilized people centuries before anyone needed to think of this other reason) is the present necessity to make the world's food supplies go further. We marvel at the work that has been done, producing wonderful vegetable synthetics including soy products; some of us may not have discovered how fit these things are, along with fresh fruit and vegetables, to be our own fare.

Besides these arguments, that might occur to anyone, the occultist and the aspirant to inner development have special self-obligations. The personal unconscious must be kept free of repressed material; not only repressed material of our own rejection, but repressed material rejected by the culture we live in. In light of this, we should reflect upon the fact that the occultist is, by the nature of his or her aspirations, committed to being at least theoretcally as self-sufficient as possible. As in less specialized cultures we should have made our own garments and equipment, built our own home and obtained our own food; we should at least be intelligently interested in, and conversant with, the processes by which all these accompaniments to our living are produced. If in some case we would not do that, could never bear to see that, then it is better for us to put that product right out of our lives.

In relation to psychic self-defense, there is more to be said. There are cases both for and against vegetarianism.

Dion Fortune opposed a nonmeat diet, primarily because she considered the custom "oriental" and therefore out of harmony with Western life and, more specifically, with Western occultism. Certainly, vegetarianism came into Western occultism from India so far as we can see; but it came first in the days of Pythagoras (sixth century B.C.E.) if not sooner, not in the days of Blavatsky; and over the centuries it has with good reason come to be associated in the Western mind with spirituality, mysticism, and wonderworking just as it has always been in the East.

Another argument, however, used by Dion Fortune against vegetarianism and since echoed by other writers, is of special interest to us here. The argument is that a nonmeat diet makes defense more difficult because it increases psychic sensitivity, so that the vegetarian has an unnecessarily acute awareness of what goes on in the unseen worlds.

If that is a valid argument, surely we should also be safer to tear out our burglar alarms and security systems? However, Dion Fortune's contention has some validity, in instances where a naturally sensitive person has already come under psychic attack. Ought he or she to cease eating meat specifically for defense purposes? No; the time of an attack is not good for changing one's eating habits, save to ensure one is getting sufficient nourishment.

There are only two instances in which we should consider a person becoming a vegetarian while actually under psychic attack. One would be if meat eating were damaging the person's physical health; the other case would be if it was seriously disturbing his or her conscience. In either of these cases, it could probably be said that the person ought to have stopped eating meat a considerable time before; but, even so, in the case of conscience we should wish to be sure it was not a device of the attacker for precisely the purpose aforementioned—to render the victim's psyche more acutely perceptive of induced images whether terrifying or seductive.

On the other hand, a person accustomed to a vegetarian diet and to the greater degree of sensitivity it confers will not be at all inconvenienced by it. Just as the eyes and the skin adjust to sunshine that an unacclimatized person could not cope with, so it is with the nervous system and the psyche. Besides—and this is important—the vegetarian does not usually attract so many negative psychic conditions or parasitic entities as does the meat-eater.

Certainly, with a nonmeat diet, it is most important to ensure adequate nutrition, both for psychic well-being and for life generally. In these days, this is much easier to ensure than it was in Dion Fortune's time; but in all ages there have been men and women who have managed it very well.

The Book of Daniel gives some interesting data, and was evidently written with real knowledge. The prophet Daniel, with the wonders that surrounded him—his prevision, and his leadership in saving his companions as well as himself from the lions and from the furnace—appears as a spiritually and psychically well-protected man and an attractive personality too. He ate no meat and his habitual diet, we are told, was "pulse," that is, such things as beans, peas, and lentils. Those vegetables are so rich in protein as to make meat eating really unnecessary.

A curious point is that later in the story, King Nebuchadnezzar also took to a sort of vegetarian diet; we are not told why, but as he evidently had developed a respect for Daniel's powers he may have aspired to develop similar ones himself. We are told only that he went "mad" and that he ate "grass." The term "grass" may originally have been meant to cover different kinds of green herbs, but, excellently healthful though leafy vegetables are, they cannot by themselves provide an adequate diet for a human being. Nebuchadnezzar's "return to nature" was evidently not a success.

The principles being understood, we have paramount reasons for recommending that anyone interested in psychic and spiritual progress, and specifically, concerned with his or her psychic self-defense (but not presently under attack) should become a vegetarian.

An important factor in psychic self-defense that we have already pointed out in this book is to avoid producing surplus energies that can escape at any level. Escaping and uncontrolled energies attract predators both incarnate and discarnate, just as sharks are attracted by blood from a wounded swimmer.

Surplus and uncontrolled sexuality can be shown to be chiefly promoted by two factors in nutrients: an unnecessarily high protein content, and acidity. (The use of stimulants—that is irritants—coffee, tobacco, and alcohol as well as heavy spices—plays its part too, but these are hardly nutrients). Both high protein and acidity are supplied by red meats, and notably also by oysters, eggs, chicken, rabbit, pork and fish, all of which are widely recognized as aphrodisiac foods.

Many vegetables, on the other hand, including notably lima beans, dried beans, celery, and carrots, are distinctly alkali-producing: we have already commented upon the remarkable property of raw carrot juice.

This should not be taken to imply that a vegetarian diet reduces the sexual powers of an individual. A glance at the animal kingdom should convince us to the contrary, even if we did not know the value of the vitamin content of fresh green vegetables in this respect. What this diet chiefly prevents is the wasting of these powers in unwanted and uncontrolled action.

Avoidance of an uncontrolled surplus of emitted energy, especially in the form of sexual energy, is essential to both men and women for the adequate self-direction of their lives. We have shown how astral vampires and other parasitic beings can be drawn to the emanations of a solitary person, and how, by taking advantage of the victim's tendency to morbid fantasy, such entities can cause themselves to be invited within the defenses of the aura. It is also a fact that these emanations of energy, or rather their accompanying signs, can be perceived whether consciously or subliminally on the material level too.

Whatever area of life concerns us, we should heed the words of an expert in that area. Mae West, besides being one of this century's greatest interpreters of womanly sexuality, was a keen student of human nature in general, with a considerable interest in psychic phenomena. Once in her heyday she was asked what a young woman could do to increase her sex appeal. Prominent among the several points of Mae's reply were the words, "Eat as much meat as you can."

Now, that was a straight answer to a straight question: okay for the girl who wants a shortcut to that kind of attractiveness, and who knows what she is getting. If she does not intend to be promiscuous, she presumably knows how to handle the situation, understanding her own impulses as well as those of the men involved.

It is not so good, however, for the girl or woman who neither has nor wishes for that kind of experience, who just wants to be as attractive as possible in the accepted meaning of that word. If she thinks of this extra meat eating in the same way as drinking buttermilk to enhance her complexion, or wearing flattering clothes, or putting a flower in her hair, she is heading for trouble. One of the causes of trouble is that since the effects of meat eating are only perceived subliminally, the responsive male, too, has little chance of conscious choice in his participation.

Besides, these subtle emanations are but a higher and less controllable octave of those we so carefully abort by means of deodorants and antiperspirants. Primitive people know this. Among the folklore of several lands is a "love-charm" with several variants: A woman wishes to gain the love of a man. She makes a spiced cake for him. But during the proceedings she passes this between her thighs, or under her armpits, or otherwise charges it with the emanations of her body. He will not consciously notice, but time and time again, this age-old sorcery works.

So the modern woman who wishes to attract on a different level, who wants to be "nice to be near" and to choose the personalities and mode of her relationships, who wants no chance of being pursued by undesirables or raped in her car—or of being betrayed by her own uncontrolled impulses—is acting in her best interests if she becomes a vegetarian.

When we turn to what vegetarianism has to offer to the male sex, the case is just as clear-cut. We have pointed out, for men as for women, the psychic dangers incurred by sexual overactivity. Regarding this state of things in context of a meat-eating population that also consumes other stimulants and irritants (for meat in its acid-producing role is decidedly one of the irritants) it looks as if men are caught in a hopeless dilemma between this chemical and energic depletion, and the psychological ills of "sexual repression."

To the vegetarian, however, this dilemma ceases to exist. Given a sane, nonmeat diet without artificial stimulants and a healthy, active lifestyle with plenty of mental and emotional interest, too, there is no sexual repression at the psychic level because there is generated no surplus sexuality to repress; while at the physical level there is a cessation of involuntary sexual activity and a consequent check to the drainage of vital, youth-sustaining products from the system. Both Eastern and Western experimentation shows this.

While there are great advantages to be gained from an altogether meatless diet, there are also benefits from frugality and avoidance of stimulants with any diet. Many people have been noted for their power over their own nature and over the external natural world, who did not adhere to any fixed diet at all: who were not, indeed, in a position to observe any rules save those imposed by necessity. To the present-day city dweller a self-imposed rule of diet is usually both possible and necessary, and where the possibility of choice exists we say frankly that a vegetarian diet is the best choice to make. However, as Laurens vander Post (for one) has made clear by his own experiences as related in his books, such a choice is not possible in all circumstances, but a considerable psychic and mystical rapport with the forces of life can still be attained if other conditions are fulfilled: especially such conditions as sparse eating, natural surroundings, and serious purpose. (If the meat-eater wants to claim justification from the explorer in the jungle or from Elijah sharing flesh with the ravens, he or she should reflect on the circumstances.)

We have known people, both city and country dwellers, who have fulfilled the conditions. In several cases, their control of natural forces has shown itself in a way that may be of interest here: the control of rats and mice.

Usually some man or woman, more or less a recluse, finds the number of his or her rodent companions has become embarrassing. So the human searches out an alternative abode for them—usually an empty house not too far away—and, with a lighthearted disregard of any conflicting human interests, tells the rats or mice about the place and bids them go thither. And they go.

That sort of thing has happened too often, and with too many witnesses, to be dismissed as either fiction or coincidence. Furthermore, a related instance of a more ethical kind is also within our knowledge.

An elderly widow lived alone in a quiet village. During the winter months, a number of mice entered her cottage and damaged her small stocks of food. Because the invaders were field mice and not house mice, she felt she should respect their seasonal needs: but although she didn't grudge them the little they ate, she did object to the quantity they spoiled. So, after thinking it over, one morning she went into her kitchen and spoke to them, "Mice, I know you all can hear me, although you are hiding. Mice, I'll make a pact with you. The food on the table and shelves belongs to me, and you must not touch it. Anything on the floor, you can have. Do as I say, mice, and there will be peace between us."

Something of this certainly got through to the tiny creatures. They kept the pact so well, that in a short time, the old lady was putting bits of cheese down on the floor to reward them, and friends who stayed with her from time to time bore witness to their good behavior.

• • •

Checkpoint

- If your working life affects you through noise, sleepiness, or accident-proneness, take a look at the material conditions and at your own lifestyle. Take a practical interest in possible improvements.

- In any case, "get away from it all" for one or more brief periods daily. Do some preliminary relaxation, and then spend up to twenty minutes communing with your higher self.

- At any time, particularly during stress or worry, close your eyes for a moment now and then for a loving, trusting "glance" inward.

- For true psychic liberation, consider becoming a vegetarian.

6

How to Survive in Business Life

Study Points

1. "Group mind" is a factor that must be considered whenever pluralities of human beings spend any extended time together.

    a. In its lesser manifestations, we can distinguish it as the group aura. It is "an aggregate emanation from all the personalities within it."

    b. Whenever the group exists for more than a temporary duration (temporary as in a theater audience), and involves more than ten to twelve members, it will almost inevitably split into rival groups.

c. Such rivalry, as in a work environment, can produce a very stressful atmosphere and even unspoken rules and bizarre games that could be imposed upon you.

2. The need for an adequate program of psychic self-defense is especially pertinent for people participating in group activities. In addition to the regular practice of the Tower of Light aura fortification, you need to:

a. Become aware of what is going on in the group—the games and rules mentioned above—so that you can be discreet and self-determined in your relations to the main group and the subgroups.

b. Always remember what your involvement in the group really is. If you are working at a job, then give the job your attention. And remember where your real loyalties belong.

3. Learn to keep your imagination under control. In a selling situation, for example, do not let the sales person's descriptions of the product's seeming advantages evoke an emotional response in you that will bypass your rational judgment based on the actual facts about the product.

a. Desire and fear are the two primary ways in which imagination can be manipulated.

Neither forms a basis for making rational decisions.

b. Conditioned behavior is another factor that can be used to bypass rational judgment. A salesperson to his or her advantage can manipulate your politeness in a social situation. Get the social factors out of the buying and business decisions. Fear of saying "No" can make your assertion of rational choice, and of individual lifestyle, difficult.

c. Typecasting is another way in which rational judgment can be bypassed. do not respond to emotional appeals directed to you in your role as a mother or father, as wife or husband, or dutiful child, or lover, etc.

d. Guilt feelings are yet another "handle" that may be used to manipulate your imagination to bypass your rational judgment. do not let anyone else ever make you feel guilty about anything—for they can then manipulate you into buying their product or service (even if it does not have a price tag—as may at first seem the case with religious people).

e. Never let fears of "missing a good thing" influence your judgment.

• • •

How, in fact, did the old lady's communication with the field mice, mentioned at the end of the last chapter, really work?

It's out of the question, of course, to suppose each of those little wild things, with its modicum of brain, could understand or make a rational decision on a speech in English. The words mattered because they enabled the old lady to direct her mind to the mice, to let them hear the different tones of her voice as she turned her thoughts, emotions, and (doubtless) her imagination to the food, the shelves, the floor, the mice themselves. They probably picked up the general feeling of all this, and the guideline of her very definite judgment. They may even have divined, in a quite wordless way, her bountiful nature a lot more clearly than she perceived it herself.

Her voice, her physical presence, and the astral level of her psyche would convey all this. The communication would not—we can say with virtual certainty—be direct with each individual mouse-psyche, but with the group mind that had brought that particular family, clan, or tribe of small rodents into the cottage as a unit.

Group mind is a very interesting phenomenon. It is highly developed in some creatures and has been exten-sively studied in, for example, bees and ants. It is conspicuous in cattle, in some kinds of deer, and in wolves. Dogs have it: it is less marked in felines, but it is present nevertheless.

Between human beings and animals—some species especially—it can be very strongly developed in certain circumstances; usually, as we have remarked, in simple or primitive living conditions. Among human beings it is, and has been, most strongly present in primitive tribal conditions, where individuality has not yet fully emerged.

In civilized life, the group-mind is recognized as being present and active when people behave as a mob. Otherwise its existence is generally ignored. All the same, individuals who have to deal with people not only as other individuals but as groups know and recognize that the group mind generally develops, for better or for worse, whenever a plurality of humans spend any extended time together.

Every actor, actress, trainer, teacher, and preacher knows the reality of the group mind. Everyone who works among other people needs to know it.

In its lesser manifestations, such as one finds in normal emotional conditions, among people who are to a great extent individuated, the group mind is more recognizable to us as the "group aura." That is the level at which leaders and trainers prefer to keep it, so they can influence and control it with reasonable facility.

It is also the level at which it tends to exist so long as the participants have normal outside interests and activities.

The influence of the group aura in the life of the individual may be either good or bad. Sometimes, for example, when a child has moved steadily up in school for a few years, always as a member of the same group, there may be a change for whatever reason (through an exam result, or a divergence of curriculum, or perhaps through the parents taking the child to live in another city). The child loses the familiar group aura, and as a result may wilt, or deteriorate seriously in morale or in health; in other cases the result may be wholly good, a sturdy developing and maturing of individuality. None of this need be the result of losing any particular friend or teacher; it may be entirely a matter of the group.

This introduces us to the subject of the group aura in the business world.

Any group aura is an aggregate emanation from all the personalities within it. Some personalities—the more "involved" ones rather than the truly stronger ones—will have a predominant share in its composition. No matter how carefully such an aura has been fostered to produce an overall "team spirit" (and also, quite often, to provide an easier means of handling people than by knowing and dealing with each individual separately), as soon as it involves more than ten or a dozen persons, it will almost inevitably be divided, as the "involved personalities" in one area may be hostile to those in another area.

This can be confusing for a newcomer, especially for a newcomer with no experience of office politics. Some firms, of course, are more afflicted with these things than others: but most of the maneuvers will be directed to getting the newcomer within the group aura, or (less openly) within the right subaura.

If one or more management-level people should happen to embark upon a real power trip, the effects on the collective aura or auras can be almost lethal. A surprising number of things develop a new significance. It can at once affect previously neutral matters such as a person's sports-club activities, or which restaurant he or she uses at midday. Among the established personnel there is usually practically no discussion of these things; just a watchfulness coupled with real subliminal awareness, and the occasional bringing into line of an unheeding junior.

A young woman who had just joined one of the account sections of a large engineering firm found the office modern, elegant, but rather lifeless. However, she'd noticed some beautiful roses on a few desks in a distant section; so next day, she brought in an armful of roses from her father's garden, just coming into full bloom, and two or three containers.

On being offered some of these roses, her supervisor with much embarrassment told her to put them all in water in the rest room and to take them home in the evening. The newcomer later learned (from someone else) that "the only person" to bring roses to the office was Mr. X, the chief rival of her own boss for a promotion that wouldn't occur before Christmas. To put roses on one's desk would be rather like wearing the election colors of the wrong candidate.

Who makes such rules? Nobody; that's the essence of the game. Someone does something in a way that is not at first noticed, or that others do not feel competent to challenge; and within days it's "understood," it's built into the aura. Mostly these things are of little importance in themselves; what governs the game is the awful seriousness of the players. The cards on the table, so to speak, may be only a matter of tennis or swimming, of roses or nonroses, but the stakes are in the group aura: who has authority, who is promotion worthy, who sets the pace, has prestige, "leads" or "edge" over the others? It can shred the nerves and can produce endless jealousies.

The most important question is, what does this kind of aura game, "atmosphere" game, do to your aura? Some people's personal aura seems to get altogether swallowed up by the emotional force of the group aura.

For instance, in the previous example, the effect of the incident upon the girl who brought the roses can scarcely have been as drastic as the effect the "atmosphere" had already had upon the supervisor.

If you find yourself in a working atmosphere that has become a dueling-ground for competing personalities, so that small matters soon have abnormal values attached to them, you may very likely need some psychic self-defense. Here are some practical pointers:

1. Perform the Tower of Light regularly; also the variant given in chapter 5 to strengthen your awareness of your higher self. This is essential for you, but in such surroundings you need to be extremely discreet about your inner life. People with a strongly developed group aura will probably sense anyway that you are a quiet "rebel"; do not give them chances to talk of, or mock, what they do not understand.

2. In everything that does not really matter to you, conform without demur. "They" think their behavior is normal. This may be because they have lost their sense of normalcy, but it's not of much help to you to be "the only person in step."

3. If you do not like or prize your job, consider leaving for a less turbulent atmosphere. If you do like and/or prize it, concentrate on excelling at it. Give it all the energy and attention other people are putting into their aura games; this will save you from being caught up in whatever astral currents they may be stirring up. Find ways to make yourself valued and appreciated. Anytime you have nothing to do at work, do not be drawn into gossipy conversation. Go offer help to a worthwhile person: but, whatever you offer to do, be willing to take all the pains in the world with it.

4. Attend to your leisure time with equal enthusiasm. Keep your sense of proportion by playing as well as you work, and getting enough rest for both. Eat sensibly, too.

5. If you aren't all that good at your job (or even if you are, if you like the idea of taking this line), counterattack. The aura game is not only for top people. Give yourself a new image (it must be something you can live with, psychologically and financially—you can't keep changing). Assert your new image. Be whatever you have dreamed of being, only more so, if possible; then do not try to gain anything by it, except the thing itself. Do not let any motives show.

You do not have to be like Elissa la Zouche, of course, although she was an interesting and successful type. She was a temp, and, as such, was always in the position of being the newcomer, the outsider, in every office she was sent to. Most temps have that experience, naturally; usually they deal with it by creating an illusion of familiarity. They walk in, say, "Hi!" as if they'd worked there a dozen times before (they probably feel as though they had) and everybody accepts them.

Elissa was different. When she walked in, you knew you'd never met her before. She was tall, bony, and blonde, with no make-up. Her clothes—she rotated three outfits—were all expensive sports classics in shades of beige and mud. It was, you somehow felt, a very great favor on her part to have come in.

Every lunch-hour she produced a pack of sandwiches and a paperback novel (the one the critics were raving about currently), swiveled her chair round to have her back to the office, and thus ate and read in solitude for five minutes less than the allotted time. Nobody dared speak to her, except about work and during working hours; and every one thought her a very superior person, capable of great responsibility. After she terminated—for quite a time after—her mistakes, blunders, and curious misuses of initiative kept coming to light; but every excuse was found, and the halo of superiority clung to her memory. In a similar emergency, she'd be asked for again.

6. Find yourself some allies if you can. If the main group in your office has a very "solid" aura, there may be several people beside yourself who do not care for it. Most likely they'll be unobtrusive folk, but very interesting when you get to know them. People of minority religions, people with strong intellectual interests either

inside or outside their job, the girl who's planning to go and embark on her real career as soon as she's saved enough money, the man who's developed an impressive range of home hobbies so he need never leave his invalid wife in the evenings: the artist, the poet, the inventor, all those who are only there to earn a living while their souls are else-where—those people will be avoiding the group aura as carefully as you are, maybe more carefully. Make friends with them; but do not try to "organize" them, either singly or as a group, unless they let you know they'd like this. These people may be loners by force of circumstance, but some of them could be loners by nature. Find out, before you risk spoiling a good friendship.

7. Do not let yourself be made to feel disloyal when you are not. Your loyalty as a worker is to the source of your pay. You owe it to that person or organization (but primarily to yourself) to keep your health, nerves, and abilities at their best. Act accordingly.

Shopping for Groceries, Shopping for a House

Whether you are shopping for something large or something small, a house, a car, or washing powder, many of the principles involved are the same. You wish to buy at a fair price if you are satisfied the article is what you want. If the article is not what you want, you do not wish to buy it at any price: even the biggest bargain is a waste of money if it's useless or an inconvenience to you.

Theoretically, the salesperson's function is to show you what you are getting, so you can reach a decision about the product and about the price. In reality, however, the salesperson's function is often seen simply as the act of selling, in whatever circumstances.

The old concept of the matter that said frankly caveat emptor (let the buyer beware) has now been to a great extent outlawed. It is not often worth a salesperson's while to make a false statement—but it may be worthwhile to tilt you into making wrong decisions.

Besides, no laws can go very far to protect a purchaser who politely agrees to buy, and pay for, something he or she does not really like or want. There is, in many instances, a "twenty-four-hour clause" suspending the validity of a signature, but considerations of distance, time, and face-saving often limit the usefulness of this. Better practice being a careful buyer, always.

How does a seller get you to buy something he or she wants you to buy? The same way you get a machine to do what you want: by pushing the right buttons.

But a person is not a machine. The first "button" that can be pushed is that of your imagination. This is all the easier to operate, because if you are to reach any decision about making the purchase, you are virtually compelled to use some imagination. So keep your imagination under your control.

If you are bidden to imagine the ease of putting a quickly prepared convenience meal on the table, take a look at (for instance) the "ingredients" panel on the package and imagine whether you or your family want to consume those things. If you are invited to imagine the pleasure of walking to your car across a grassy expanse on a summer day, imagine also what it might be like on a winter evening. Beware of listening to long rhapsodies, or eloquent word tapestries. They aren't woven for entertainment; they are snares for the imagination. Even if you do not see what they are aiming at, cut them short.

A notable judge was once hearing a murder case; a rich woman had left a substantial legacy to the doctor who for many years had attended her, so her irate relatives accused him of killing her. As it chanced, the weather while the trial was on became very hot, and as sultry day succeeded sultry day a good many people in the crowded courtroom, including the jurors, became drowsy and inattentive. The prosecuting counsel embarked into a long peroration, describing how, according to his case, successive doses of narcotics had been administered, so that the patient, feeble, weak, and exhausted as she was—(here the lawyer's voice became soft and slow)—far from protesting or wishing to protest—gently lulled by the sleep-inducing drugs, slipped gradually, and peacefully . . .

"Speak up please—I can't hear you!" the judge barked unexpectedly. A score of slumping bodies jerked up guiltily. The prosecutor went on to finish his speech, but the spell was broken. The doctor was duly acquitted.

So, if anyone embarks on a long, vivid description of your children's rosy future if they have the latest dictionary to help them through their studies, or how the car you just want for getting to work each day could, if you choose the right one, convey you on vacation to the breathtaking scenery of—you love mountains, do you not?—bring the conversation quickly back to facts. You can fill in all the pretty pictures for yourself.

Two powerful ways of manipulating the imagination are by the levers we have previously noted, desire and fear. Remember, your imagination is subrational; it connects with your emotions, your instincts, and your physical senses, but it does not connect directly with your rational mind. The two examples just given, your desire for your children's success or your love of mountain scenery, are characteristic of how the imagination can become confused when dealing with a salesperson. What is it in fact that you are buying? Think.

Desire and fear, when they work together, can produce a powerful "pressure" toward a sale. Maybe the thing offered to you has, as you see it, good and bad points; the price is fairly reasonable, the object is in some ways attractive, but is the condition all it should be? Maybe you say you would like to have someone else look it over.

Then the seller says something like this: "If you want this house (or car, or whatever) you'll have to decide right away. I have got another prospective buyer for it, and I cannot hold up the sale."

Again: think. What reason has this person for favoring you? If someone else offered to buy the merchandise, why wasn't the sale clinched? Or is the other prospect in fact hesitating? Then ought you not to hesitate too?

Yes, you certainly ought to. More than that, the existence of that "other prospective buyer" is very, very doubtful indeed.

Another button that can be very effectively pushed with many people is the politeness button.

The preamble to the sale of any commodity of reasonable worth is likely to be conducted on a social footing. That is the case in most parts of the world, but unless you are completely "at home" in that situation, it can lead to your deciding (wrongly) that this is not the time to ask vital questions about the object under consideration, especially if the other party keeps the conversation focussed on other topics.

Feeling at home in any situation does not depend upon having been in that situation before. It depends upon your feeling at home in your protective aura; and this in turn may be largely dependent upon your accustomed consciousness of it.

(Occasionally it is the other way around. Sometimes, a person who has always been the perfect mouse will suddenly find himself or herself in some crisis or emergency, and will never be a mouse again. But, most people are either born with inner confidence or they have to work for it.)

In your home life, in your working life, wherever you find yourself, take every opportunity to experience courage and confidence in your protective aura.

So do not be afraid to take the lead in the conversation. Take it right out of the seller's hands; if there are points you want to discuss, questions you want answered, now's the time. Socially, this may not be the best of manners—but this is not a social occasion, it's a business occasion in disguise. Get it out of its disguise. Cut right across the probable banalities.

Glance at your watch if you like, start in on your questions. Usually, if everything is okay, the seller will be quite happy that you take this attitude. Remember, he or she may be nervous, too, and may have been making small talk out of diffidence about coming to the point. But do not be sidetracked again.

Food is a weapon that can be used to attack you on two levels together. Eating is very much tied up with your trained-in notions of politeness and what is due to one's host. It can also weaken your resistance, especially if you eat with good appetite, by inducing a plain instinctual reaction of goodwill toward the giver. (Hence the importance and insidiousness of the business lunch.) This, again, operates in both great transactions and small ones.

You wouldn't let (for instance) somebody selling you a house take you to lunch and then treat the deal as settled. But that is practically what happens sometimes in the business world. Generally, lunchtime euphoria has been responsible for strange decisions.

Similarly, if you are buying your groceries, chances are you left home early to have plenty of time and to get the best bargains. Then, just when you are feeling a bit wilted, there's a girl in a crisp uniform giving out substantial samples of something that (usually) smells good. You accept—why not?—and stand rather self-consciously nibbling while she delivers her patter about high vitamins, low calories, or whatever. As you finish your snack, she hands you a package. Do you just say, "Thank you—I'll take two," without looking any further?

Read the label carefully. Think. Before marketing any product, a manufacturer makes sure there's a public for it; but does that public include you or your family? If you decide to buy—fine. If not, you can just put the packet down again (remember that). You do not owe the saleswoman anything. But better still, if you can, when you have put the package down, tell her why you aren't buying. Most of these people have been trained and briefed so whatever you say will be quoted back to the manufacturer. You may not be the only person to say there's too much sugar in it, or you never buy anything with that preservative, or nobody in your home eats whatever-it-is. She'll not be offended; you are doing part of her job for her as well as (in the long run) a good turn to yourself and your family. These reports make for better products in the future, foods that are more as *you* want them.

Another push button you can very well do without is the typecasting button. Can you be appealed to emotionally as a good wife or husband, a good son or daughter, a good mother, or even as a good lover?

It's good, it's wonderful to be any of those things; but to be typecast as one of them can make you a target for exploiters of all kinds.

They will assume you have stopped thinking in that particular area, and will just respond emotionally to the appropriate stimuli; and even if this is not at all true, they can make it embarrassing, difficult, or almost impossible for you to get decently out of that particular net. You have to keep your mind clearly on the facts, your knowledge of the real people involved, and of yourself.

Would your husband appreciate your buying yourself an outrageously sexy negligee for his birthday? Would your wife be "thrilled" if you gave her a really extravagant piece of jewelry? Does your mother really like being taken out to dinner on Mother's Day, or does she just think it's a good mother's duty to accept that sort of thing? Your answer to any question may be either "yes" or "no," but your money and your life are both involved with your knowing and being aware of the true answer in every case.

There are no ends to the possible variations on this theme. For instance: a salesman is showing the mother of a young family over a house. "And, let me see, Ms. Kindly, you have three children, do not you? You'll appreciate the kitchen—all finished in stainless steel and white enamel, perfect for hygiene!"

She may really agree, or she may not. She may believe a bright, home-like atmosphere is more important for children than clinical hygiene. But, because children have been brought into the discussion instead of her having been asked simply for her opinion on the kitchen, she may, if she is not careful, feel emotionally confused, guilty, or at least embarrassed about disagreeing with the salesman: he has inferred that a "good mother" *must* agree with him on that point.

But of course it was no part of his plan to ask her opinion at all. He just wanted to get her to say "yes" to that kitchen.

This brings us to a final point, which is really the most important point, on this whole question of sales resistance.

There is a type of salesmanship—not a very sensitive one, but very successful—that just consists of getting a person to accept something, whether the "something" is the thing they'll be paying for or not. Even if no individual is going to try to sell you anything, it's as well when you go into a store to take conscious note of the prevailing conditions, because these may be the things you are going to be accepting when you buy the merchandise. Is there any music being played? Is there an appropriate odor? Tinted lighting? The more pleasing these things are, the less likely they are to be unplanned. They are part of the reason why you are more likely to find the merchandise more acceptable there than in other stores! They are part of the glamour world most of us, at heart, want to believe in.

Not all stores that do these things sell shoddy merchandise. Some of them have high quality goods. But the customer pays extra for buying them in an atmosphere of luxury.

The real reason these things work is the same as the reason people hesitate to ask the questions that are so vital in a private transaction; why the stay-at-home parent feels compelled to buy the food he or she has sampled; why the professional salesperson is so keen to start you agreeing with him or her. From childhood onward, we are all conditioned against saying "No" to anything. It's impolite to say "No." It's unkind to say "No." Later on, you gather you may damage someone's ego if you say "No." People develop a positive superstition against saying "No." It's an "unlucky" word—if you say it to A, B may say it to you. You can evade, but not refuse. If you do not want to go to the party, you must say "Yes" and then try and develop an irrefutable excuse for not going. (One woman solved the problem by keeping by her a scent-spray she knew she was violently allergic to. Twenty-four hours before an unwanted date, she used it; and every person who saw her after that, told her firmly to stay in bed. She suffered genuinely, acutely, and miserably; but it was worth it to her.)

People who go on a diet wonder why they meet with so much hostility from their relatives—parents especially. Usually the hostility is directed, consciously or not, against the diet that gives the dieter an excuse to refuse things. To refuse an article of food is taken as rejection of the person who offers the food; so the dieter has, at least, to be made to feel thoroughly guilty about it. Why is not the parent proud to have a strong-minded child?

To recall the word "No" from its low status as the answer to a question might be a major step to a saner, stronger, and more honest state of society.

There are occasions when a firm "No" must be said, and if not earlier, then later; so it's of no use to give a soft answer and hope the problem will go away.

One type of such occasion occurs when you have done a favor to a person once, maybe twice (like doing some unpaid overtime at work, or letting a relative make decisions about your life), and then you find that instead of being a rare emergency, it comes to be considered as a regular thing, and you are no longer asked if you mind.

You have no alternative but to put your foot down firmly, without delay. Probably nobody will deny you are only claiming your rights; the offenders may accuse you of hurting their feelings (never mind what they did to you.) but you can consider this a sign of your coming victory. Be strong.

Quite a different type of occasion when you have no alternative but to be completely firm, is when you have to deal with someone who does not want to take "No" for an answer. Some types of religious proselytizers are like that; people who come to the door and want you to buy and read their works on religion, or to attend a service at their church.

If you are not interested, you should make this quite clear at once. If you start feeling it is not nice to be abrupt with someone who wants to talk about God, you'll find it quite difficult to get rid of them. It usually is useless to say you'll drop in at their church and then simply not go, because unless they are a very large, busy organization they'll give you a follow-up visit.

The reason why you have to be firm with them, is that these religious people usually have two lines of approach. One is that of charm and friendliness; the whole thing is on a completely person-to-person footing, so that if you delay too long in telling them you aren't interested you will have another bad case of hurt feelings on your hands. You won't like being abrupt with a gentle, friendly sort of person, but best get it over quickly.

Their other line of approach is to make you feel guilty. No matter why—guilty about your rejection of them, guilty about something in your past life, guilty about anything or nothing. A number of churches can only handle newcomers who have some sense of guilt. That's the other reason why you should get rid of them quickly—before you get to that stage.

Professional gamblers you may chance to meet while traveling also rate a firm "No." Do not give reasons, but do not hesitate. Then there can be neither argument nor persuasion. Do not act as if you feel sure you would be cheated or robbed; your answer is no, and that's all they'll get. They probably will not waste much time over you.

The trouble about gamblers—and about some other people we have to mention—is that people often hesitate too long in rebuffing them, not from a plain fear of seeming impolite, uncouth, or callous, but also from a deep, secret fear of maybe missing a good thing. Do not worry about that. Nobody becomes a professional gambler for the fun of going hungry, and they certainly are not in it for the pleasure of filling your wallet, either.

Fear of missing a good thing is one of the reasons, too, why women so often try to cling to dead-loss lovers of all sorts—or rather, let these cling to them, for in such cases it's the men who hang on. Pity is another motive; many women have been told by psychologists that they should always let a man down gently. There are occasions when self-preservation should come first; besides, if the woman wants to be "kind" to the man, she should recognize she'll have to send him on his way in the end, so it's better not to build up his illusions.

These dead-loss lovers are much of a kind: the man who keeps a woman on the fringes of his life, or refuses to take central place in hers, who won't let her tell her friends they are dating; the born rover; the man with a long chain behind him of terminated jobs or terminated marriages, or both. There's nothing but grief in accepting the company of any of them; but if not dealt with firmly, they'll cling like burrs.

Fear of missing a good thing can lead to even more serious trouble with another sort of people: tricksters, charlatans, or anyone whom you have reasonably suspected of taking dishonest advantage of you, or who seems to be offering you too great a return for whatever they want of you.

A notorious con man was being sentenced, when the judge said to him, "You have broken the laws in a way that cannot be condoned, but there is one thing I consider an injustice. You ought not to be standing in the dock alone. Those who were your victims have also been in many cases blameworthy; they only fell into the traps you set for them, because they themselves were trying to evade the law or to obtain something that was not justly theirs."

There is truth in that. Those feeble rejections of persons or influences we do not want in our lives—how often are they due simply to fear, how often also to some degree of desire? Desire for a glamour we know to be false, desire for a benefit we know to be spurious or illicit: the gambler in us responds to the gambler in the outer world, and is fortified by the concept that "No" is not a nice word anyway. This may seem a severe judgment, but this is a book on psychic self-defense. It is not about fun, or how to gamble in life, but how to be safe at all levels. The real fun is when you are safe.

• • •

Checkpoint

- If you work in a very "clannish" atmosphere or one much affected by ambitious people's power trips, concentrate on your work. That way you guard yourself from your destructive environment, and no one can complain of it.

- If you like the idea of "hitting back," stop blending into the background. Start your own personality trip. Dramatize yourself; assert your new image.

- Find allies—but do not try to organize them into a group of your own.

- Remember, your loyalty to the firm you work for does not require involvement in office politics.

- When shopping, go on doing your own thinking and directing your own imagination. The mere fact of wanting to buy something puts you in a potentially vulnerable position. Carefully examine any fears or desires that are put to you: you need to base your decision on facts and reason.

- A sales session is not a social occasion, even though it may be dressed up to look like one. Do not be reticent with your questions. When you mean "No," do not fear to say it—even to the "nicest" people. Do not be typecast into a role allotted to you by the salesperson.

7

Strengthening
the Defenses

Study Points

1. The spiritual and the material worlds are not
   separate: they are conjoined by the mental and
   astral worlds.

   a. Things and actions in the material
      world can be made to produce
      special effects by nonmaterial
      means.

   b. Symbolism and ritual can thus add
      force to an original object or act.

   c. An *amulet* is an object that by its
      shape, composition, or origin is

suited to be the focal point for a spiritual force, and made yet more effective by invoking a divine power to accept it as a channel of influence. Such an amulet can be a helpful aid in psychic self-defense.

2. For warding off danger ritual has the highest value.

  a. Rituals can bring in the power of a group for greater strength in protection of either group members or a single person.

  b. Rituals can also be performed by one person, directing a special protective power against the source of danger.

  c. The first eight psalms can be used in a special rite for invoking a divine blessing.

3. Some people seem to have more than their share of bad luck. It may be that someone is "jinxing" them, or even more likely that they are unconsciously jinxing themselves.

  a. It is feelings of guilt in the personal unconscious that are the most likely source for such bad luck.

  b. You can, and must, get rid of guilt feelings. Forget about rewards and punishments. Be true to yourself. Commune with your higher self, and know that you are loved by that divine presence.

  c. Expect success in all your endeavors. Positive anticipation invites success.

• • •

Many people recognize two dimensions in life: the spiritual and the material. These two dimensions, however, are often conceived of as being quite separate from each other. Thus (for instance) to pray is seen as an act related to the spiritual world, to eat one's dinner as an act related to the material world.

The mystic and the occultist see these things in a different light. People adopt special bodily attitudes for prayer, we perceive, partly because having any special attitudes fixes the mind on the special act, and partly because the traditional attitudes have their own symbolic significances.

Likewise, eating one's dinner has spiritual as well as physical connotations. Many religious people say grace as a thanksgiving for the food and a reminder that even earthly benefits have a spiritual origin. A number of occult-minded people use another formula, declaring that the body is nourished so that it may fulfill the purposes of the spirit.

The spiritual world and the material world are not in that sense separate and we are only robbing ourselves of life-potential if we try to divorce them. Between the material world and the spiritual world, we know, lie the great astral and mental worlds; but these participate, from one to another, in so many related qualities that we can say the astral and mental worlds conjoin the material and spiritual rather than parting them.

It is because of this intermingling of influences that human life is full of examples of symbolism and of ritual: things and actions in the material world that are intended to produce an effect by nonmaterial means. Some of these things are very powerful. Occultism is largely concerned with the study and application of these methods; that is, it is concerned with the occult (hidden or nonapparent) significance of things and actions that, in themselves, are plainly manifest to the senses or to scientific instruments.

Often the original significance and force of a suitable action or object can be raised to a much higher potency, or to a higher octave altogether, by adding something significant. Thus, a symbolic pouring of water on the body is intensified in power if the action is accompanied with suitable words of purification or dedication (as in baptism). An object which, by its shape, composition, or origin is suited to be the focal point of a spiritual force can be made more effective by—blessing—it (invoking a divine power to accept it as a channel of influence), by engraving a special symbol upon it, or so forth. Of course, the closer the relationship between the material, the symbol, and the particular aspect of divine power that is invoked, the more effective other things being equal—we can expect our "amulet" to become.

Amulets, as a matter of fact, are a relatively minor department of psychic self-defense. They are given some special consideration here, firstly, because their use is such an ancient, widespread, and well-organized area of human activity, and secondly, in one form or another they truly help many people. They give people a focal point for their aspirations and their confidence, a reminder of the ever-presence of the high powers to those who revere them; and not an empty reminder either, because the amulet must in its nature and in its shaping (if any) be something that the power in question can take as a channel of operation.

In the Greco-Roman era there was a fashion, revived at the Renaissance, of having exquisitely wrought figures of classical deities engraved upon its appropriate gemstone. Thus, a Hercules or a Mithras, solar heroes, might be represented upon a topaz; a Mercury or simply his healing caduceus upon a carnelian; a Diana upon rock crystal, a Venus upon ocean-born, magnetic amber. Artists capable of beautiful work of this kind have always been rare, and for the special purpose of gemstones as amulets such elaboration is unnecessary. To have the planetary symbol engraved on the appropriate gemstone, however, would be a good way of identifying it as an amulet, with more character and force than the "birthstone rings" usually seen at jewelers; those, of course, if similarly prepared, should have the zodiacal sign engraved upon them.

After the work is completed, a simple but serious "clearing" of the stone from all negative influences and a dedication of it to the appropriate power, with a statement of intent where appropriate ("for good health," "for happiness in love," "for success in study") could complete the making of this type of amulet.

Lists of stones for the zodiacal signs are often seen and are very variable: the planetary stones are less commonly given. Here, too, alternatives are valid; but based upon traditional considerations the following is a sound list. Moon: rock crystal, beryl; Mercury: fire-opal, carnelian; Venus: malachite, jade, amber, coral; Sun: topaz, zircon (white or blue), goldstone, tiger-eye; Mars: garnet; Jupiter: lapis lazuli, amethyst; Saturn: onyx, jet. If the stone is to be put in a setting as an amulet, the corresponding metal might well be used to add force to the whole, but it would for various reasons not be advisable to wear some of these metals habitually in contact with the skin.

The planetary metals are as follows. Moon, silver; Mercury, a white alloy (not silver or tin, but essentially a mixed metal; perhaps an aircraft alloy.) Venus, copper; Sun, gold or brass; Mars, iron or steel (including stainless steel); Jupiter, tin; Saturn, lead.

The art of making talismans, whether of stone, metal, parchment, wood, or other substances, suitably inscribing them and then charging them so that they are truly infused with the appropriate force, is a process of knowledge and skill, too complex to be completely dealt with in this book that has so many aspects of psychic defense to cover.

Sometimes you don't want to go in for elaborate methods. Sometimes you just feel your general luck has soured on you. You need a fresh start, something to carry you round the next corner, something to give you new confidence.

So you might go find your amulet, in the Native American way (study the traditions). Go out into the country, find a rocky place, mentally review your problems, and lay them before your own high powers. Then you look for a small pocketable rock that catches your attention in a peculiar way. The longer you've been in the open air, the better you will be at this. Much can be learned from books about Native American tradition, but you need the living "feel" of it. When you find your rock, take it home—don't let anyone see it. Wrap it carefully and keep it about you. Also ponder over any ideas that came into your mind in the course of that expedition.

A variety of materials have entered into the traditional usages of psychic self-defense, frequently as supplementary aids to stronger techniques. Asafetida, iron, silver, and other things can be useful if rightly applied according to the rules of a particular tradition, but are not essential to anyone's general psychic well-being.

Salt is a powerful cleanser and a first-rate antiseptic. From ancient times it has also been used in ceremonies to carry the idea of cleansing on the nonmaterial levels too; and there is use for such cleansing. Thus, by tradition, even though plain water itself also carries the idea of purification, a little salt is added when the water is blessed for ceremonial use. The salt fulfills the purpose of cleansing the water from any adverse influences it may have absorbed in this natural state, so that the blessing and whatever dedication it receives can have their full effect.

Whatever materials are to be used, whether for an amulet, or talisman, or in carrying out a serious ritual act of any kind, a cleansing and setting-apart is desirable first. If there is any doubt whatever of a thing's past associations, a Breaking of the Link ritual (see page 118) should be carefully carried out.

For psychic self-defense proper, however—that is, for warding off danger whether general or specific—ritual methods are of the highest value and power.

The rituals described below are supplementary to those given earlier in this book; for psychic safety, nothing can take the place of the development of the aura. The ensuing rituals are basic forms for defense that, with only varying details, are known and treated by people of the Western tradition in many lands. They are given only in outline, so that the person or group using them has maximum freedom to bring in a specific symbol, divine name, or method of working. The Walls of Light visualization is not easy, but is of very great worth and merits practice.

A group performing one of these rituals should, unless the members have great psychic attunement, choose a leader from among their number. The leader's task will be to coordinate them, to cue them in, and to speak a few lines solo.

The first ritual we describe is a potent method for a group to use, either regularly or on an occasion when strong psychic protection is desired for all members. Each one fortifies his or her own protective aura within the walls of light; the individual auras can be pictured as overlapping like the haloes of a cluster of lamps seen through a mist, but they do not merge. Each person is thus doubly protected, both as an individual and as a member of the group.

Group Ritual for Psychic Protection of All Members

(Powerful protection for a group that feels in any way threatened; for people in a house troubled by an apparition or poltergeist, for people meeting with unexpected problems while on vacation, for a family or group disturbed by noisy, hostile, or overcrowded neighbors, for a family who want their unity blessed at the close of a reunion, or as a regular goodnight ritual for friends who lose sleep through nervousness; for any plurality of people who want to share and to strengthen their psychic protection.)

1. Stand in a circle, facing center.

2. Link hands, each person giving the right hand palm downward, the left hand palm upward.

3. Leader states agreed purpose of the ritual; for example, "We join in this circle—for the safety, health and peace of mind of us all"; "for a quiet night"; "for divine blessing and protection upon our unity"; "that we may reach a solution to our problems"; etc.

4. Each member of the circle builds up in visualization two walls of light enclosing the whole circle of people: the first wall of light, a high wall of white light with sparkles in it of bluish-silver, is only slightly outside the human circle. This wall of light revolves clockwise. The second wall of light resembles the first, but is just slightly further out and taller, so the upper edge of the second wall appears over the top of the first. The second wall of light is revolving counterclockwise. (This formulation of the two walls of light and their movement is not an easy one, but it is a very valuable and powerful defense. Beginners should concentrate on getting the inner wall clear first. The revolving is likely to be experienced as only a slow movement at first; the

objective should be to speed up the movement of both walls with practice.) Ample time should be allowed for all members of the circle to visualize the walls of light.

5. Unlink hands.

6. Each member of the circle performs individually the Tower of Light, regular method; the leader can indicate the successive stages if desired.

7. Link hands as before, to reestablish the circuit between the members of the circle. As this is done, a surge of power will rush through the people in the circle, counterclockwise (because each person is giving with the right hand, receiving with the left). The more sensitive participants may be able to feel this circling of power as an objective reality; but everyone alike can help greatly, knowing it is there and imagining it flowing ceaselessly around.

8. Make jointly a solemn declaration, invoking blessing, spiritual power, whatever is needed for the intended purpose. (Leader may cue the others in).

9. All join in visualizing a previously agreed divine symbol, in brilliant light above the center. All spend a few moments in contemplation of this, then together chant several times a divine name (or attribute, such as "holy wisdom," "love," etc.); at the same time, visualizing the symbol getting even brighter, shedding radiance on all. To conclude, a suitable valediction is pronounced.

(*Note*: The greatest force is gained when the name or attribute, and the visualized symbol, are related: as, life everlasting with the equal cross or the ankh; Holy Spirit with the dove or the flame; Sun of Righteousness with the Star of David or the Byzantine eightfold star.)

A group may perform a variation of this ritual for one person whom they wish collectively to protect spiritually.

Group Ritual for Psychic Protection of One Person

(A group may wish to give maximum protection to another person who is especially threatened by psychic attack; or maybe a family wants to give special protection to one who has been physically ailing, or to a young child.)

1. Stand in circle, facing center; person to be protected is at center.

2. Link hands, as described above.

3. Leader states agreed purpose of the ritual.

4. All together visualize the two walls of light surrounding the entire group, as described above. Then two similar walls of light are to be visualized surrounding the person in the center, the wall nearer the center revolving clockwise, the wall further from the center being slightly taller and revolving counterclockwise. (The person at the center, if able to help in the visualization, should do so.)

5. Unlink hands.

6. Each member of the circle performs individually the Tower of Light as indicated above. (The person at the center, if able to perform this also, should do so.)

7. Link hands, reestablishing the circuit of power.

8. Make jointly a solemn declaration, invoking blessing, and whatever is needed for the purpose of the rite, upon the person at the center. (Members of the circle do not in this variation invoke a blessing upon themselves.)

9. The visualized symbol above the center, and the collective chanting of the divine name or attribute, are just as described above; except that during the chanting, light is visualized as streaming down only upon the person at the center, and is contained within the inner walls of light. Conclude with an appropriate valediction.

The following ritual procedure is intended for one person to use, in such an emergency that even the emergency method of the Tower of Light needs to have time found for its performance. This is rarely necessary but it can be done.

Rapid Emergency Defense Procedure for One Person

1. Stand facing the direction from which danger is apprehended.

2. Visualize your special sign of spiritual protection (cross, circled cross, pentagram, Star of David, or

other) in brilliant blue light. Visualize it in the center of your forehead, as strongly and brightly as possible.

3. Raise your arms in front, the backs of your hands facing you. Bring the tips of your two forefingers together, and the tips of your two thumbs, so as to form a triangle.

4. Raise your two hands together so that the backs touch your forehead, this triangle framing your visualized symbol. Pause for a moment thus.

5. Utter (silently or aloud) a divine name so that its power may activate your visualized symbol.

6. Suddenly, violently, fling out your arms before you, hands parting, and fling the visualized symbol forth with that gesture, toward the menace. Visualize the flying symbol burst into a blazing brilliance—and you will have your space to perform the Tower of Light emergency method.

The ceremony that follows is not strictly a rite of psychic defense, but is a means of invoking divine blessing. It can be used at any time but it is primarily an evening rite, and, as will be seen, on the occasions when it is performed it most effectively precedes the Tower of Light formulation.

It will be recognized by some as a type of working used in certain traditional Qabalistic lodges. It owes its potency to the ascent which the serious participant is enabled to make to the world of Supernal Spirit, so as to infuse the psyche with that divine force: this is brought through for protection and well-being at all levels, in the ensuing Tower of Light.

The especial secret of Psalms 1 through 8, that are recited in this rite, is well-known to Qabalists; this sequence of Psalms makes the ascent of the Sephiroth from Malkuth to Binah. Expressing this in more popular terms, these Psalms relate to the "spheres" of Earth and the Seven Planets in their Qabalistic order:

Psalm	Sphere	Sephirah
1	Earth	Malkuth
2	Moon	Yesod
3	Mercury	Hod
4	Venus	Netzach
5	Sun	Tiphareth
6	Mars	Geburah
7	Jupiter	Chesed
8	Saturn	Binah

Psalm 1, for the Earth-sphere, gives the image of the just man as a flourishing tree, and the wicked as wind-blown chaff. Psalm 2 opens by showing "people imagining empty things," illusion being one of the well-known characteristics of the Moon-sphere. Chiefly, however, this sphere represents the power of generation in all its aspects, and Psalm 2 also has the key utterance, "Thou art my son, today I have begotten thee."

Psalm 3 well reflects the sphere of Mercury, the sphere of healing and divine protection. The sphere of Venus, repre-

sented by Psalm 4, is the domain of the joyous and innocent Nature-forces; hence, the likeness of the emotions, the
blessings of natural abundance, and of hope.

Psalm 5 celebrates the sphere of the Sun, which Qabalis-
tically is the Sephirah of divine manifestation to the lower
spheres. Here we have reference to the temple and to
human entry into the abode of deity; with the pronounce-
ment that the Lord will dwell among those who trust him.

The next sphere is that of Mars, and in Psalm 6 we find
a plea for exemption from divine wrath. Psalm 7 balances
this with its account of "God the just judge, strong and
patient"—fully befitting this Jupiterian sphere. Finally
Psalm 8, for the sphere of Saturn, celebrates divine power
as being "exalted above the heavens," and links heaven and
earth in a superb glance downward from the Sephirah
Binah as Mother and Giver of Form, through the themes
of Tiphareth and of Malkuth; the visitation of God to man,
and man's dominion over Earth with its diverse life-forms,
all considerations proclaiming the God-given dignity and
elevation of humankind.

It is interesting that this same sequence of Psalms that
makes up the First Kathisma (division) of the Psalter in
Byzantine usage, still forms a part of the Orthodox Office
of Vespers.

The Rite of the First Kathisma

(This can be performed by one person or by a group; very
well by two.)

For this rite, eight lamps, candles, or floating wicks are
required. If votive lamps are used, there is this advantage:

cups of colored glass can be obtained if desired. If all the lights are plain white, no harm is done: if colored candles are used they will have white flames anyway. But the correct colors for the eight lamps are as follows.

Saturn—indigo, a dark neutral tone, or smoked glass can be used.
Jupiter—blue
Mars—red
Sun—yellow
Venus—green
Mercury—orange
Moon—violet
Earth—white: Earth receives the influences of the whole spectrum.

If the lights are being arranged on a holder with different levels, the highest place is allocated to Saturn; but they can very well be arranged in order horizontally. (A small ordinary candle placed near by, alight, and with a taper, may be a convenient aid.)

Open the rite with an invocation to the Most High. This can be in your own words, or in others that attract you; it should be fervent but not lengthy.

Next, read Psalm 1, slowly enough to let your mind and imagination dwell on the words. At its close, light the lamp that represents the Earth-sphere.

After a moment's pause, with similar thoughtfulness and imagination, read Psalm 2. At its close, light the lamp that represents the Moon-sphere.

So proceed through the eight Psalms and the eight Lamps. When all the Psalms have been read and all the lights are burning, make another short, reverent invocation of the Most High.

Let there be another brief pause here, so you (and every other person participating, if others be there) can catch something of the feeling of the divine presence to which you have been raised by this ascent. Then conclude with the Tower of Light.

The Forward View

In looking to the future, for general, long-term psychic self-defense, the higher spiritual levels are important. We should always feel we have reserves beyond the ability to cope with a present emergency.

In this regard, bodily life, business life, and the life of the psyche have close parallels: the people we call "lucky" are generally the ones with resilience, recuperative power, with the resources to achieve the goal of their efforts.

Most of us learn early in life that a fair amount of physical pain or emotional stress is well worthwhile, if the suffering is incidental to achieving some goal we really want. What matters in such a case is achieving the goal, not avoiding the suffering.

If a mountain-climbing expedition succeeds, nobody says, "Those poor guys, what a lot of hardships they endured," although maybe they endured plenty. Everyone (including the climbers themselves) says, thinks, and feels, "They're lucky, they made it!" Everything else is swallowed up in that.

In same way, when you see a pregnant woman, you may feel a lot of compassion for her. But later, when you meet her with her new baby, you feel happy, you congratulate her. It's the same principle.

Men and women have struggled onward to whatever, in the context of their own lives, spelled "success," even against adversity that would have made many reasonable people declare their task impossible. These men and women succeeded because inwardly they knew it possible. They had faith: some in one thing and some in another, but all believed in the goodness of their goal and their ability to reach it.

At the same time, we must recognize there are some people who have more than their share of "bad luck." Ill health, family problems, money troubles, disappointments of one sort and another seem to single them out. They seem to be "jinxed" and that's just how they feel. The result of all they do is frustration, despondency, and often bitterness.

Someone may be jinxing them—or they may, more likely, be unconsciously jinxing themselves. Either way, they are involved, because another person couldn't "get at" them unless their aura was in a bad way, or some hidden level of their psyche let the harm through.

Put your aura and your psyche right and you can laugh at all jinxes, hexes, and curses of any kind.

But why should anything in your own psyche be loading the dice against you?

These things can happen for various reasons, but here is one of the commonest: guilt.

It makes little difference what you may or may not have done. We are dealing here with your personal unconscious, not with the great collective unconscious that transcends your conscious personality. The contents of the personal unconscious is usually a very miscellaneous collection of influences and impressions that have fallen into it through the sieve of memory all your life; and there can be some quite mistaken emotions and impulses in the bag.

One of the most tiresome and harmful kinds of delusory influences that can lurk there is the one known as "free-floating guilt." That is a tendency to feel guilty, or to react as if guilty, about anything or nothing, or about everything.

To illustrate: a new kind of "lie detector" was recently tried out, in laboratory conditions. The tests were well-planned, but the results were not altogether satisfactory.

Certainly the device screened out the "guilty" volunteers. No "guilty" person succeeded in producing an "innocent" reaction. But, it also registered a number of "innocent" volunteers as being "guilty." Their nervous systems had reacted just as if they were "guilty."

Even though all these people knew (i) that this was only a laboratory experiment, and (ii) they weren't even "guilty" within the terms of the game, a certain number of them, just because they were being questioned, couldn't help registering "guilt" from a submerged level of their psyche.

Since, however, so many people react in a guilty way without cause, we begin to understand how in other circumstances people will accept suffering as punishment, equally without cause. This is true in the case of curses fairly frequently.

So if you think you have been hexed, jinxed, or just plain unlucky, don't even waste time considering whether you "deserve" it or not.

Forget about rewards and punishments. Both are beside the point, false views of your relationship with the spiritual world and, above all, with your own higher self.

The true relationship between your higher self and your lower self (the latter includes your conscious personality) is love. It is real love. No divine judge is ever going to trip you over something in your past that you may or may not remember.

If you look into your past, look so as to gain understanding of yourself; never mind praise or blame.

For the present and the future, strive in all your decisions to be true to yourself—to the best and highest you find within you—and expext success in your actions.

Commune often with your higher self on the lines of the method given in chapter 5: and remember, it's you whom that divine presence loves, not anyone else's idea of what you ought to be.

If you want a symbol to remind you of your aims and aspirations, make one.

If you want to tell the high spiritual being who governs your life that you have faith in your destiny, then do that. If you feel you need protective rites or a rite for divine blessing, this book has them.

Strengthen your defenses, and within those defenses make, step by step, your own inner life. Complete sincerity among all levels of your being is the best psychic self-defense possible.

· · ·

Checkpoint

· If you feel you need an amulet, make one, or go find it.

· Any material or object to be used as an amulet or talisman, or in carrying out a ritual, should be given a special "cleansing" and "setting-apart" according to its purpose.

· Study the group rituals so you with your family or friends can use them any time they are needed.

· Practice the Rapid Emergency Defense. This is an extremely powerful defensive gesture, using whatever may be your special sign.

· Always follow the Rapid Emergency Defense with the Tower of Light emergency method. That way, you are practicing two excellent things in short time.

· The Rite of the First Kathisma is the only one given here that needs any equipmen—the Book of Psalms and eight lights. You might want to make sure you have these things by you.

8

Retaliation and Growth

Study Points

1. Psychic attack is much more exhausting than psychic defense—hence good defense can outlast any attack. You do not need to retaliate in order to end an attack: the attacker will have to give up, eventually, if you keep your aura strong.

    a. Knowledge of your own instinctive reactions to attack is helpful. With this self-knowledge, your reflex actions can be programmed to employ the techniques of psychic

self-defense instinctively, even without you
ever knowing of an attack.

b. With a well-developed aura, any adverse
force will "rebound" from its outer edges—
returning the attack to its source.

c. Sometimes, however, a decisive act to end
the attack may be desirable.

2. Why does another person attack you? If this person
desires to harm you out of malice, jealousy, vindictiveness, etc., surely his or her psyche is in need of healing.

a. "Bless them that curse you, pray for them
that maltreat you." To bless effectively will
heal your enemy's sickness of soul, and
end the attack for good.

b. Your higher self is a spark of the divine—
hence you have the power to bless.

3. The aura is part of the whole person. And, because the
psychic aura and the electrical aura are themselves parts
of one whole aura, the strengthening of the psychic aura
will in turn strengthen the electrical (or health) aura.

a. Psychic self-defense—the strengthening of
the aura—is thus important to physical
health and well-being.

b. Psychic self-defense—because the well-
developed aura is not only protective, but
radiant—is likewise an important means
to helping and healing other people with
whom you are in contact.

c. Psychic self-defense opens the door to awareness of the spiritual world, and the awareness and communion with your higher self is one of the most important steps you can take in this life.

• • •

Self-defense of any sort is a subject that tends to involve our emotions; this applies to psychic self-defense as to the rest.

From a practical viewpoint, the natural emotional approach, if controlled, has value in speeding up the necessary reflexes for our safety; but if uncontrolled, it can plunge us into needless dangers.

How can you employ your emotions and instincts to your benefit, without placing yourself at their mercy?

Part of the answer is, by familiarity with the emergency methods so you can reasonably expect them to come coherently to mind if required. But, above all, it is vital for you to sort out, in calmness and at leisure, your basic attitude of mind.

What is your chief emotional reaction in a hostile situation—fight, flight, or something else?

Is your predominant tendency to run away, to be angrily aggressive, or to stay put and try to outwit the enemy? None of these attitudes can be called simply "right" or "wrong."

It all depends on circumstances. The reason for this bit of self-examination is not for you to give yourself praise or blame, but just for you to find out which of these attitudes you are most likely to overplay, given a situation in which you have to make a snap decision. Armed with this knowledge, you can build "balancing" considerations into some imagined situations, and play with them mentally to get the feel of behaving in a way that may be novel to you. This does not mean going against your basic temperament, just learning to be a bit more fearsighted and flexible about it.

Flight is not always a shortcut to safety. Your attack need not always be frontal. Guile needs knowledge, first, of the enemy.

This leads to the subject of retaliation, which frequently does not seem an expression of vindictiveness, so much as a prudent followup after foiling an attack. The less confidence a defender has in his or her ability to go on with a prolonged psychic conflict, the more concerned he or she will be to find some definitive, perhaps violent, means of ending it early through fear of becoming exhausted.

That seems reasonable, but it fails to take into account a peculiarity in the nature of the matter. Unlike many other forms of combat, in psychic combat attack is out of all proportion more exhausting than defense; especially since some good defense methods (such as are given in this book) can, indeed, revitalize the defender.

Knowing a serious attack to be exhausting, the occultist or sorcerer who is an experienced psychic attacker is likely to put every effort and art into terrorizing, bullying, and bluffing the defender into an early capitulation, which the defender, however inexperienced, need not grant: it is the attacker who has genuinely to fear a prolongation of the conflict.

To make a disabling retribution is thus less necessary than the beginner in psychic self-defense might suppose; and if it is not essential, the questions arise, is it ethical, is it worthwhile, is it desirable?

Those who fear it may not be ethical are likely to have on their minds certain New Testament phrases on the subject of "turning the other cheek" and "returning good for evil." We shall in fact need to examine these phrases rather carefully, because putting them in a context of psychic self-defense helps to bring out their true meaning.

With regard to any type of attack, psychic or otherwise, a possibility of making retaliation needs careful thought.

Is the matter serious enough to warrant retaliation? If the attacker seems to have been trying to "teach you a lesson," probably not; if he or she was reacting from a punctured ego (a usual case) you do not have to show signs of the same trouble yourself; your best course can be to strengthen your defenses and then simply to ignore the incident.

If it is a serious matter and you do retaliate, will this ensure finishing the matter or prolonging it? Quite likely the latter; if you do not return the attack, the attacker will in any case have to recover energy after making it, and could after that lapse of time decide not to try again. That often occurs; good defenses discourage further attack, pique fades, new concerns supervene. But if you on your side deliberately renew the conflict, you are inviting a further attack; and this time it may be your assailant, tired of it, who decides it will be best to finish it quickly and violently. Certainly, your defenses can still be good; but to live continually in expectation of sudden reprisals is unpleasant.

These are the kinds of considerations that sometimes prompt occultists to stop a foolish occult feud by the "shock absorber" method: that is, by simply digging in, strengthening their defenses, and refusing to react until the assailant retires bored. That is quite a good method so far as it goes; but it achieves nothing positive, and for most occultists, achieving something positive is a necessity of life.

So let's see what the New Testament teachings have to offer us.

Anyone interested in understanding the meaning of biblical quotations should always take care to look at them in their context. The very well-known words on "turning the other cheek" in fact follow, and are a part of, the important injunction (Luke 6:28) "Bless them who curse you, pray for them who maltreat you."

First of all, it is noteworthy that this advice on "turning the other cheek" can be presumed not to be meant too literally; it is, then, a figurative use of words, meaning only "do not react" or "do not retaliate." When Jesus himself, the speaker of those words, was struck on the face (John 18:23) he did not turn the other cheek, but very reasonably asked, "Why do you strike me?"

"Bless them who curse you, pray for them who maltreat you," however, tells us much more. That is the important clause. If you bless and pray effectively, what will happen to your adversary?

If another person's desire is to harm you (as by a curse), his or her psyche needs healing, and blessing. Bless effectively and that sick tendency to aggression and malice must certainly disappear, perhaps for a short time, perhaps forever. You will have done your enemy nothing but good but you will have removed that enemy from your path.

Supposing on the other hand you were to curse some person who, by psychic attack or other means, was working evil against you? You would be adding your anger and malice to those of your adversary, so you would very likely receive the impact of both. (If a fierce wild animal is pursuing you, you gain nothing by enraging the animal.)

So, how do you bless?

A blessing is a wish, given in the name of (that is, in the power of) a divine being. You can use whatever divine name or title you really believe in; as your higher self is the divine spark within you, you can validly and powerfully say, "In the name of my higher self."

All such names have great power.

If you can visualize the person you are blessing as enclosed within his or her auric shape, the person and the shape becoming irradiated with light as a result of your blessing, that will make it truly potent. Otherwise, it is just a "good wish."

You can make it a general blessing, or you can bless a person for good health, for prosperity, for patience, for any quality you believe to be needed. But take heed: it must be for something you really think will be for that person's spiritual growth and good; otherwise the contradiction may set up a block in your unconscious mind, which could destroy the operation.

(Bless your friends, too, your family, your home.)

If you can in this way, bless someone who has tried to attack you psychically, the force of his or her malice must dwindle before the active splendor of your higher self. However, you may not feel you are required to deal with that person in this way.

A more usual defense, and one that, quite often, you will not even know about when the defensive shield of your aura is well developed, is the rebound that occurs to any adverse force that impinges upon its outer edge.

All influences, whether good or bad, have a natural tendency if they are repelled by their intended recipient, to return to their source—the person who sent them out. Quite frequently, in the case of a recipient in good psychic condition, the rebound is spontaneous and usually those people have no awareness of most of the influences their aura repels. Sometimes cultists, however, will deliberately send a psychic charge or current back to its source in this way, either just so as to free the victim from it, or as a punishment—a "slam-back" to punish its misguided originator and to warn him or her, effectively, not to do it again.

When such a charge has been sent maliciously, to cause sickness or unhappiness to the recipient, the effect upon the originator of it when it has been slammed back, can be a most exactly matching retribution. When the intention was not malicious but selfish and unconsidered, the effects can be more variable. An example of the latter kind is given in chapter 4.

Let us not, however, in the last pages of this book, dwell unduly upon the harm human beings can cause to each other whether intentionally or through folly. There would be enough to do in life, and sufficient need for the basic techniques of psychic self-defense, if no such troubles had to be dealt with.

Those who are growing to adulthood need to develop and strengthen their individual aura; those who have been weakened by sickness or infirmity may need help in repairing their defenses.

Our aura, like our skin, is an organic part of healthy living. Because the psychic aura and the electrical aura are parts of one whole rather than two separate things, the strengthening of the psychic aura is also an important adjuvant means by which we can work on our physical health and well-being. Indeed, the more deeply the researchers look into the causes of ill-health of many kinds, the more significant do they find negative conditions and emotions to be problems that were in the environment of the sufferer and that have done their damage without anyone intending or knowing it.

Radiant self-confidence, a sense of your ability to cope with the emotions of others, the power to follow through with your own plans and purposes in the midst (if need be) of chaos, capacity to help others without yourself becoming mired in their despondency, their fears, and troubled imaginings: all this new power at your disposal is among the fruits of psychic self-defense.

There may be, too, a new awareness of the spiritual world, a new realization that you are a part of it just as certainly as you are a part of the material world and of the other levels of existence. To establish an awareness of your higher self is one of the most significant and important steps you can take.

Conscious of your natural and valid defenses, you will be able to outgrow hidden fears and inhibitions, able to cast away old grudges and resentments. Some of these things may disappear without your even having plainly known they were there—but the awareness of liberation from them will be yours no less distinctly. Let this be so. do not cling to the past or brood over it: move into your new, bright future.

• • •

Checkpoint

- Sort out your basic reactions in situations of any kind of danger: not simply what you would wish to do, but also try looking back to what in the past you did do. This is where imagination can come in, to suggest adaptations for the future.

- Practice blessing.

- Continue with the Tower of Light and building up a real relationship with your higher self.

- Sometimes practice your emergency procedures.

- Realize psychic self-defense as an integral part of normal, positive living.

Appendix A

Defending An Enterprise

Once you have mastered the principles given in this book, you can bring the high, protective power of psychic self-defense very effectively into action, whether for one person or for a group of people in a number of widely varied situations.

In this appendix we are considering a use of psychic self-defense that is in some ways distinctive, and this can give you further pointers for its application in yet other circumstances. What is to be looked at here is the defense of an organization or enterprise: a business, an educational, or religious endeavor such as a college or church of whatever kind, a nonprofit organization, in fact any banding together of people for the attainment of some purpose outside their family life.

The examples given here differ from some that have already been considered, chiefly in one important particular: the enterprise is not totally identifiable with the assemblage of the people involved in it.

Even a family business can have needs for protection that differ to some extent from those of the people whose fortunes are bound up with it. Any enterprise, generally speaking, may need protection from envy and slander without; from the development of some form of disloyalty or self-seeking within; it may need protection from the efforts of rivals and imitators. It may need protection from that indefinable quality called "bad luck" that frequently results from a lack of "goodwill" on the part of the public, or a lack of judgment or good timing on the part of the decision-makers; or simply from "forces beyond your control."

For instance, you might start a completely legal and honest enterprise, intending it for nothing but good purposes. Then some other group of people, taking advantage of a loophole in the law, might organize something unacceptable and scandalous, provoking new legislation that might inadvertently cut across your project. Or you might patent some gadget to meet a long-neglected need, and have everything set up for its production; at which point another firm might bring out—and advertise extensively—a machine to achieve the same result more rapidly.

There is no way such accidents can be prevented—unless by psychic self-defense. How, then, do you set about it?

The first requirement is that you should keep your own protective aura in top condition by regular use of the Tower of Light (pages 45–47), besides maintaining a healthy, positive attitude in your life. If the enterprise is principally yours, this is a main contribution to its defense; but in any case, you should, if possible, have whatever other "key people" there are in it adopt the same measures. Although in the action of psychic self-defense it is often possible for associates to bridge the gap created by a "weak link in the chain," obviously it's far better that there should be no weak link. If your associates do not believe in psychic self-defense or do not think they need it, then this makes your own action even more plainly of paramount importance.

If you and your friends are in the process of formulating a new enterprise of any kind, you would do well to obtain some astrological guidelines for choosing the day and time of its inauguration. The intended purpose of the enterprise will need to be taken into consideration; also its location, and the natal charts of its key people. If you can also make out a list of days and times when the official inaugural meeting—the actual "birth" of your enterprise—could reasonably be held, this will further help to simplify the astrological work.

If possible, before that meeting, work out a timetable of events, an outline of aspirations, or a contract, whatever may be suitable. When the meeting takes place (whether you have been able to schedule it astrologically or not), begin by performing the Tower of Light through step 8 (pages 45–47), but expanding your visualization of your aura so as to encompass the whole meeting. (Remember, your real aura can do this without difficulty: it is only your customary visualization that needs to be enlarged.)

If you have to sign or to resolve upon a decisive document, take it—being aware of the new extent of your aura—look at it and say within yourself such words as: let the beneficence of the light be shed also upon this ... (corporation, association, work, whatever). Proceed with step 9 and, when you have completed it, maintain your visualization while you sign or resolve upon the document. When you have handed it back, perform step 10; step 11 follows at the end of the meeting. Should the inauguration not be a matter of document-signing or resolving, then use this same technique to give a blessing to the enterprise at whatever may be the critical moment: but keep the whole meeting, or the operative part of it at least, within your extended protective aura. The procedure given here indicates the general principles. Naturally, it should be adapted where necessary to fit the particular needs of the case.

When, at the end of the meeting, you let your visualization fade from awareness, you should know the new enterprise remains in truth where you have placed it symbolically within the bright shield of your protective aura.

Visualize it so, often, in the early days of the growth of the enterprise. Represent the enterprise in your imagination by any symbol you find most fitting: its logo, or the building that houses it, or any object that typifies it; "see" it as present with you, within your aura, and bring down the light of your higher self upon it in blessing. Make a regular time daily, in connection with your Tower of Light, for this short meditation.

The matter, however, cannot and should not rest there. Just as a child can only be protected within the mother's aura until the child's developing individuality has emanated its own aura, so your enterprise, too, must come to maturity. The best gift you can give it at this stage is to help develop the independent protective aura it will need.

This is no fanciful analogy. Failure to take this step (whether visualized or not) has proved fatal to many an excellent project, no matter what capability on the part of its first originator may have led to that failure.

Take care, therefore, to ensure that the success of your enterprise shall rest on a broader basis than that of your ability or your personality. Think of the part played by your associates, and by the public; think of all the adjuvant circumstances you can. Do not be grudging about this. You need not fear: what you have done will remain yours even when you have "weaned" it from you, and it will be all the more robust and enduring for the separation.

As an example, consider the history of human flight from the first imitators of birds' wings to the landing on the moon. Each inventor's vision, however dated it may be now, keeps a lasting fame because of its relationship to the rest. Or consider Shakespeare's plays. People now find these to be mines of philosophy, of sociology, of psychology; but initially they survived because they were actable and were acted, with all the acting talent, stage management, and theater organization this implies. Whether you are a philanthropist, an engineer, a realtor, or a restaurateur, if your enterprise is to go forward, it needs not only to keep its identity, it needs to keep that identity while being carried by the activity and the imagination of other people besides yourself: other people, too, besides your immediate associates.

Therefore, when once the initial stages of formulating your enterprise are safely completed, turn your own imagination creatively to the varied factors that will further the growth and advancement of the work.

Begin building these factors into your daily meditation upon the enterprise: pass them in review, visually, if possible, when you have completed step 9 of the Tower of Light; then perform steps 10 and 11 as usual.

After about a week of this procedure, and on a definite occasion decided upon by yourself, after you have performed the Tower as far as, and including, step 9, visualize the enterprise (represented by your customary symbol for it) with all these adjuvant factors present with it: you can on this occasion identify each factor in turn without giving it any prolonged attention. Then, "see" the enterprise as becoming surrounded by its own shining, protective aura—an ellipsoid of bright blue light—that is supplied partly from your own auric material but that is emanated partly also by the enterprise itself and partly by the adjuvant factors.

When you can clearly visualize, or be clearly aware of, this field of bright blue light entirely surrounding the representation of the enterprise, you should visualize within the summit of that aura, a little above— not touching—the symbol, a globe of brilliant white light.

Concentrate your attention on this globe so that it becomes brighter, glowing white like burning magnesium. The initial source of this radiance is the light of your higher self; but you should call to mind that it also represents the real link that the enterprise itself has with the higher powers, as a focal point of energy, imagination, and thought that has come into being on the material plane for a good purpose. Thus, although this globe is a visualized symbol, it represents a part of true divine force. The divine sanction of our endeavors is a complex subject, that need only be briefly glanced at here. It is difficult to conceive of any activity that does not serve, or has not been set in motion for, some good purpose; equally there are few activities that do not, or may not, cause some degree of harm. These degrees of good and harm have to be taken into account if the worth of an activity is to be weighted: obviously one person's view of the matter may differ from another's, and some people's views may, one way or another, be inordinate. In the present context however, you simply have to decide what—in the light of your own aspiration, love, and sanity—is the "good purpose" that gives this enterprise its rightful place in the universe.

If you see in your enterprise a specific potential for harmful use, you can use the method of protection given above to prevent this from developing.

When you feel ready, "see" that dazzling globe sending down glittering white light, flooding the aura and completely permeating the symbol of the enterprise. The outer shell of the aura remains sharply defined as an ellipsoid of intense bright blue, all filled now with the living, vibrant, sparkling white light.

Continue this formulation for some time, the brilliance flowing down ceaselessly into and around the symbol and circulating, effulgent and sparkling, within the hard, outer shell. Then let it fade gradually from your consciousness, being aware at the same time that it has not faded from reality; the reality of the enterprise continues to possess its own protective aura, newly fortified by the supernal light.

Having done this, complete steps 10 and 11 of the Tower of Light in the normal way for the full-scale visualization you have done for yourself.

You may wish to repeat the above procedure of endowing the enterprise with its own aura, during one or two further meditation sessions; after that you should consider the protective aura of the enterprise as an established reality that, certainly, you can help fully reinforce from time to time, not failing to visualize and to affirm the support given thereto by other people and circumstances also.

Another good way you can employ psychic self-defense on behalf of an enterprise is to adapt, for the premises (factory, clubroom, office, shop, clinic, whatever) used for its activity, the technique for the home outlined on page 52. Vary the words to suit the use of the place: for instance, "May this door be blessed for the coming and going of loyal members, and may their number increase; but may it bar all envy and contention from entering." Or, "May this door be blessed for the coming and going of good customers; may they enter to purchase with confidence and goodwill, and going away may they recommend us to their friends. But be this door a barrier to frown upon and turn away all pilferers." Of course, ensure that on the material level you have an adequate security system. Think in terms of crime prevention at every level. But material means alone are not always adequate.

This is an excellent procedure in itself, and it will be the more potent as you clearly visualize, or imagine, the various positive circumstances for which you are asking. It also gives you a pointer to a variety of important ways, going outside the proper scope of psychic self-defense, in which you can very positively gather strength and power for your enterprise. "Helping Others See Your Vision" is the subject of appendix B in Llewellyn's *Practical Guide to Creative Visualization,* which comprises vital aspects of creative visualization for all who are in any way concerned with putting their ideas before the public.

Suppose the enterprise in which you are interested is long past the initial stage of development? Or suppose you are not the chief person involved in it? (It might simply be the business in which you hope to work until you collect your pension, or the church or club you regard as your "spiritual home.") In any such case, this present appendix should suggest a number of ideas you can use to contribute to the psychic defense of the enterprise, both by your own individual action and by psychically "inviting" other people to do likewise.

Any enterprise, if it is to grow and prosper, needs to catch the imagination of a host of people, many of whom will be far removed from its inaugurators. No matter whether you are its first originator, therefore, or whether you are one of the later comers, you can do vital work for it: making brighter and more attractive, stronger and more enduring, its image and its protective aura in the astral world.

Appendix B

Psychic Defense Against Crime

A t different points in this book we have suggested the very real value of psychic self-defense
against various types of criminal activity: violence,
fraud, theft. Here are some further vital ideas and
effective methods for the defense by psychic means
of yourself, your family, and your neighborhood.

You, or one of your neighbors, may ask, "Psychic self-defense? It is excellent for the uses mentioned earlier in this book. But when it is a
question of my property—or of my children—I
want protection by solid physical means."

Of course you should use the material means available to protect persons and property against crime. But psychic measures, for their own special uses, are also indispensable and should not be neglected.

Here are two examples: you have your own house. You are planning to go on vacation, and you mean to have your place continue to look "lived in" while you are away. You made sure you had all the luggage you needed a while back, and you bought timers to turn lights, etc., on and off in your absence, thus avoiding a last-minute parade of vacation-type purchases. You have discreetly arranged to stop deliveries while you are away; and a good friend has promised to collect the mail daily from your curbside mailbox, to pick up any packages left outside and to ensure no telltale circulars are left in your screen door.

Everything will be okay if your friend does these things. But accidents happen. Conceivably, some startling news might cause him or her to forget; or sickness or some other emergency might make the promise impossible to keep. What more, then, can you do?

You can notify your local police or sheriff's office of your intended absence. That is a good idea in any case. And you can further protect your home with psychic self-defense.

Or supposing you have just moved into a rented apartment. You plan to have a deadbolt lock fitted to the front door, but then you find the door itself is so weak, no lock can help you until the door has been reinforced or changed. Your landlord agrees to take care of this for you, but can't have it done at once. So what do you do meantime?

If you are not already a member of Operation Identification, you'll do well to join it. Find out about it at your police office. Mark your stealables as instructed, give a list of them to the police, and put up the appropriate stickers. Never mind the advice some people may thrust upon you, against "putting up a notice to say your things are worth stealing." Once your possessions are identified in this way, for the great majority of burglars and other thieves they are not worth stealing.

Besides this, give your property the extra protection of psychic self-defense.

The first essential in almost every variety of psychic self-defense is to keep your own defensive aura bright and energized, and for this we recommend regular practice of the Tower of Light. Even in methods that do not specifically involve use of the Tower, this practice is of immense value in protecting and empowering you. So do the Tower of Light regularly, and protect your home frequently by the method given on page 52. But this is only a fraction of what you have the psychic power to do in preventing crime.

It is difficult to show evidence for some things. You can say, "So-and-so has practiced psychic self-defense for thirty years, and in all that time he or she has never been robbed"—but how do you know so-and-so would have been robbed had it not been for that practice? So-and-so, you may be sure, is not concerned with that question. He (or she) is content to live unrobbed, be it consequence or coincidence, and will assuredly continue the psychic program that goes along with that happy state of things. As Crowley says, "Who hath the How is careless of the Why."

Leaving aside the question of robberies that fail to get committed, however, it happens that circumstances have in one instance revealed the "inner workings" of a simple procedure that can be very effective in protecting personal possessions. We do not say the working of this technique would in every case follow the exact lines described here; the real point of this history is that it shows the technique itself operating potently, and in a way that goes beyond the range of coincidence.

In a city whose stores were splendid with cosmopolitan wares, lived a woman who (like many others) had cultivated her tastes more effectively than her resources. Often she was, perforce, content merely to admire the beautiful things she saw displayed; but occasionally she would resolve upon a purchase. If she couldn't at once buy the article she decided upon, she performed an inconspicuous little rite: a form of the "Claiming Technique" that will be described below for your use in safeguarding your property.

(This technique is a basic magical method that, with slight adjustments to the accompanying words, visualizations, and ways of thinking, has been used through the ages to bless, to set apart, or to dedicate people or things to any special purpose or ownership. You, too, can adapt it to other and varied uses if you so desire.)

The woman of whom we are talking would just rest her hand for a brief while upon the object she had chosen, inwardly affirming with full confidence that it was hers and nobody else would or could buy it; if for some reason it was impossible for her to touch the object, she would instead simply rest her gaze on it with the same resolution. Over and over, the article she chose in either of these ways would remain in the store, sometimes for months, until she could buy it. But, of course, she usually had no idea what reaction caused other shoppers to pass it over.

One day, a friend who wanted to give her a present asked her what she'd like; so she described a beautiful Venetian vase she'd resolved upon a couple of months previously. The friend made an expedition to get it—the store was in another part of the city—but came back with the disappointing news that the vase was gone. She and the sales clerk had searched the store: there was no vase answering to that precise description, although there were others not unlike it. The odd thing was, the clerk didn't remember its being sold; but the only possible solution was for the two friends to revisit the store together and make another choice.

As soon as they entered the store, the woman who had willed to own the vase saw it—the very one without a doubt—on a shelf facing the door, quite plain to see. She pointed it out, and it was thereupon bought for her; but both the friend and the clerk were positive that particular vase hadn't been there the last time they had looked.

It may have been invisible to them; more likely, it had merely seemed "irrelevant"—a curious magical "conditioning" by which both things and persons can escape notice, often in the most seemingly impossible circumstances.

You can protect your treasures from the covetous in the same way.

Your physical body is your primary instrument of living in this world. Hands, feet, eyes, ears, every organ that enables you to give expression to any faculty, or fulfillment to any desire, gives you in its measure a special mode of living, a way to extend your power of being.

Each material object that you own and value must be in some way also an extension of your means of living in this world, and thus an extension of your physical body. It must be an article of use or of delight to you, or both; or you intend that it shall be so in the future. You would do well therefore to "claim" it as such, to charge it with your living energy even as your physical body is charged.

This is said so that you may understand the very deep and intimate level of feeling with which the necessary action is to be performed. It is like the way an athlete may pass a hand over his muscles before a contest, or a woman may stroke her beautiful hair while she brushes it. These actions express no mere "pride of possession": the physical attributes in question give their owners a means of expressing a very real part of the inner self. That is the way it can be, and the way it rightfully should be, with your feeling in regard to your prized possessions.

To ensure employing with full effect the technique we are discussing here, you should be doing the Tower of Light regularly; and for at least a week you should have employed it morning and night. Then assemble together, or sit conveniently in relation to, your possessions that you wish to "claim" protectively.

Place yourself consciously in the presence of your higher self, by performing completely the procedure given on pages 128–129.

Having done this, take up and handle, or rest your right hand upon, each in turn, of the objects you want to protect in this way.

Be aware that you have, in the middle of each palm—corresponding roughly to the sensitive triangle formed by the heartline, the lifeline, and the mount of Luna—a center of activity which, though relatively "minor," is very powerful in the giving and receiving of psychic energy. You should be sure, therefore, either to hold the object so as to send a psychic current straight through it from palm to palm, or to place the center of the palm of your right hand directly on top of the object so as to impel the power forcefully through it. (The right hand gives, whether you are right- or left-handed.)

Really think what the object means to you while you do this, and say—aloud or silently—"This is mine. I send my life-force into it to protect it, because it is part of my life." Withdraw your hand(s) gently after completing this.

In this way, you consecrate the object to your own use and delight.

However, protection of your own home and possessions is not all that can be done by psychic means. If you have friends and neighbors who are interested, or whom you can interest in psychic self-defense, you can do a great deal toward helping stop crime in your neighborhood.

Maybe the idea of psychic self-defense might seem far-out to some people in circumstances when they do not feel it's urgently needed; but if an emergency comes up such as a wave of vandalism, fire setting, or purse snatching, or attacks on children or seniors, your neighbors might see the need to do something about it at the psychic level as well as materially.

Whether you get a sudden outbreak of crime or not, a "neighborhood watch" is no bad thing. Its organization must depend largely on the type of neighborhood yours is: large isolated houses, closely built high-rises, a business area that is more than half deserted after office hours, or so on. Your local police or sheriff's office is the best source of advice for yourself and your friends if you want to organize something useful on the material level. But here are a few psychic—and psychological—pointers:

Apart from the relatively rare case of the monomaniac—a psychopath who is "preprogrammed" and is not likely to be influenced by whatever you do—a lot of protection can be given to potential victims by lifting them out of the "victim" class.

Old people and children alike get conned (and worse) by "friendly" strangers who offer sympathetic help the victims weren't looking for. So stage one in protecting them is to ensure your children and your senior friends and relatives know they aren't "out on a limb"; they have their real friends and neighbors and do not need anything from strangers.

Stage two—a very important one—is to turn children and seniors, when possible, into responsible members of the campaign by giving them their part to play in their own protection and perhaps in that of others. How active a part each plays must depend upon individual temperament, ability, and inclination; but most children over seven can be taught to notice what is happening around them as they are coming and going, while even older folk who can't get outdoors generally enjoy looking out the window, and the more active can be around while other people are at work.

The chief point is, whether or not any of the youngsters or oldsters ever help detect or prevent a crime, they can learn some very important lessons for their own protection: to "walk tall," always to have evidence of a definite errand when seen in public, and to look purposeful as they go about. To those counsels can be added this: never, if it can be avoided, have a perfectly regular timetable.

The avoidance of a completely fixed routine not only protects the walker: it also tends to unnerve the would-be lawbreaker. Two old veterans with a keen, alert expression who used to patrol their block at unpredictable times soon cleared the area of loiterers, even though—a fact that wasn't generally known—neither of them could see with any certainty more than about four yards ahead!

At the same time, you need to impress upon your patrols—the kids particularly—that if they do see anything suspicious, such as people of any age tampering with parked cars or with unoccupied buildings, they should just unobtrusively withdraw at once and take whatever steps they have been told for reporting the matter. They shouldn't attempt any amateur sleuthing themselves. That way, you will prevent their running into personal danger but at the same time keep them behaving as, and living as, responsible people: not as unaware, potential "victims."

Besides all the methods already described or suggested in this appendix, a number of techniques given earlier in this book are valuable in communal defense against crime. The strong aura of the individual is the basis of each method. If several families in a block practice the Tower of Light regularly, they will gradually build up a protective "communal aura" for the block, whether they are conscious of it or not. You may, however, desire to add swifter and more specific methods to this.

The "group ritual for psychic protection of all members" (pages 176–179)—the primary Wall of Light method—is intensely powerful and thoroughly merits the initial effort to gain proficiency in it. Besides the variation given on pages 179–180, the "group ritual for psychic protection of one person," a further variation can effectively be used in which two or three pairs of parents, aided perhaps by a few relatives or friends, place their several children in the center of the circle for protection by this means.

Whatever is done, it is essential to develop an atmosphere of confident and intelligent self-help, not one of fear or anxiety. If your neighborhood has a real crime problem, or a youth problem, or if there is a feeling of depression due to the number of derelict buildings, for example, the psychic and spiritual atmosphere becomes particularly important for everyone. If you and your friends can't meet every evening, you might consider meeting once a week to join in the strong and inspiring Rite of the First Kathisma (pages 183–184) which, based entirely on the Psalms, may transcend many differences of faith: it is very potent for protection, cleansing, and peace.

Beside these measures designed directly to protect people, you and your friends can also take vital measures to protect the locality itself. The actions you perform can be effective at two levels simultaneously, and these you will do well to bear in mind; since an effect deliberately intended is generally more powerful than one simply caused by performing the right actions without realization. There are two levels of adverse influences:

1. The quiescent level—that of the many materials such as rock, brick, cement, wood, which are to a greater or less extent capable of recording and preserving the influences of strong or often-repeated emotions projected upon them.

2. The active level—that of such elementals as have been corrupted by human contact, and that often lurk at sites of habitual crime or vice. As described earlier in this book, these elementals not only batten upon energies released in sexual or alcoholic overindulgence, but, to obtain further supplies of energy, by means of morbid illusions will prompt their victims to further excesses. Sometimes, too, these elementals become aware of the even greater release of life force that results from bloodshed; and then, fanned by their promptings, jealousy, or drunken anger (for instance) can assume a sudden violence, whether homicidal or suicidal, for which no real cause is seen.

The effects of these adverse influences, whether at the quiescent or at the active level, exist in the astral world: that is, in the world of emotion, of instinct, and of fantasy. If you and your friends seek to combat these effects at their own level alone, you have no real or lasting ascendancy over the forces you oppose. You must bring in the power of a higher level before you can claim any "moral advantage." Before setting out on your protective tour of the locality—for such a tour is needed for effective action—you and your friends, assembled together, should each perform the Tower of Light. This can be done simply or, better still, all can join in the "group ritual" given on pages 176–179.

Should you and your friends wish to pray together on this occasion, that is excellent; whichever ritual procedure you have chosen should then follow your prayer, so that the high spiritual force with which you have attuned yourselves may reinforce the power of each person and of the group.

There is no need for your tour to be made in the darkness of night, but you should be aware which places are after dark the desolate yards and alleys, the lurking-places and the meeting-points of loiterers. If there are any known sites of actual crime, especially of repeated crimes, give special attention to these.

Give special attention, too, to any point on the road where a bad accident has occurred. A moment's fantasy or illusion can betray people into bloodshed much more easily by a road accident than by getting them to commit a crime, so this can be "elemental" action too.

At each point that you and your friends decide upon for special attention, you should all simultaneously perform the Claiming Technique that has been described above. This is a part of your neighborhood, the district in which you and your children have the right to live, your lives free from the fear of any molestation of soul or body. You claim this place in the name of the powers of light accordingly. If there is an obvious place on which members of the group can rest their hand—the post at the entrance to an alleyway, or the door of a deserted building, for instance, this should be done; those of the group who are not in a position to do this should rest their right hand on the shoulder of one who is touching the post, etc., or the members of the group may form a chain in this manner.

For this special use of the Claiming Technique in cleansing a locality, no matter whether the Wall of Light method was used earlier or not, the members of the group should now all link hands, right over left; there is no need to form a circle, and so the people at the ends of the line(s) will each have an unoccupied hand. You, or whoever is acting as the leader, should say quietly on behalf of the group, "For the cleansing of this place and the protection of all who come here, we claim it in the name of . . ."

Then all join in uttering a previously agreed divine name or attribute, and visualize a divine symbol, as described on page 179; the light from the symbol entering into the place to be cleansed. (If there is no symbol on which you and your friends would all agree for this use, you should all visualize a sphere of white light and speak, "In the name of our higher selves" or "Of divine love.")

After a few moments, the group allows the visualization to fade from consciousness, and moves on.

If there are many trouble spots in your locality, it may need more than one expedition to deal with them all. In any case, your group should repeat its visit after not more than two weeks, and again if need be. This is, however, a very potent form of blessing.

Crime is a problem that has to be met effectively at every level: spiritual, mental, emotional, and material. Necessarily, in giving suggestions regarding the other levels, we have referred to the material level of crime prevention too—but that is not really the subject of this book. As we have said on another topic, "Whatever area of life concerns us, we should heed the words of an expert in that area." On the subject of crime prevention, the police or the sheriff's office are the experts. They can't redesign your home for you or live your life for you, but if you want help or advice they can either give it or tell you where to find it.

For the rest—remember that besides being an individual, you are a "cell" in a larger living body: the community in which you live. That community is a psychic entity as well as a material one, and you have your part to play in keeping it healthy. Even if it were possible or desirable for you to live without exchanging a word with any other person, you would still have that responsibility; and you could still in some measure fulfill it. A genuine air of happiness and confidence as you go about does not only help protect you; it gives real help to other people too.

It helps older folk, or people with troubles, to remember life is still worth living, to straighten their shoulders and look about them with new confidence. It helps youngsters (who often have their own fears and anxieties) to know that their seniors can look on the bright side, because it is not each person against the world.

And if we have fewer malcontents of all ages, more joy, and more love, will this not mean less crime?

Glossary

Amulet

Any object worn or carried for the purpose of warding off harmful or negative influences.

Archetype

A universal concept as conceived in the divine mind (Philo, Augustine) or in the collective unconscious mind of humanity (C. G. Jung).

Astral bleeding

Involuntary loss of astral substance, usually from the solar plexus region.

Aura

A natural emanation of energy given out by a living being. Psychic aura, the forcefield that emanates from the astral body; electrical aura, the forcefield that emanates from the physical body.

Centers of activity

Energy-centers of the astral body, corresponding to neural or glandular centers in the physical body: the "chakras."

Dream diary

Record of dreams, usually for analysis or to examine the responses of the psyche to a given program; in connection with psychic self-defense, the purpose is to detect symptoms of a psychic attack and its nature.

Elemental

A "nature spirit"; one of the living beings of the astral world, less individuated than human beings, sub-rational, but highly sensitive, reactive, and mimetic.

Forcefield

The area in which a particular energy or influence operates. Alpha forcefield, the electrical aura; beta forcefield, the psychic aura. (See **Aura**).

Glory

In art, a halo or nimbus, especially one surrounding the whole figure (as of Christ) and shaped as a conventionalized aura.

Halo

In art, a disc or circular area of brightness about the head of a divine or sacred person, representing the light from the highest center of activity.

Inhibition

A veto set up by an unconscious and subrational factor in the psyche, forbidding the person to think of or recognize certain facts or instincts, to perform certain actions, etc.

Instinct

A subrational, innate, and usually unconscious impulse that prompts living beings to react in given ways to certain situations that are critical in their lives: distinguished as the instinct to seek nourishment, the instinct of self-preservation, the mating instinct, etc.

Kathisma

A division in the Byzantine Psalter.

Mandorla

An almond-shaped area or panel enclosing a sacred figure, and representing the aura in medieval Italian art.

Meditation

A state of thought or of inner contemplation in which, by using the imagination, by concentration, or other means, attention is turned entirely away from the outer world.

Nimbus

A bright "cloud" of luminosity mentioned in classical literature as surrounding the figure of a deity when seen on earth; in medieval art, a brightness surrounding the head of a divine, saintly, or royal personage.

Occultism

The pursuit or study of that which is "hidden"; of knowledge and powers not evident to the senses or to scientific measurement.

Poltergeist

A "noisy ghost"; usually a manifestation of much uncontrolled energy, with knockings, hurled or transported objects, activity involving fire, water, etc. Frequently of human (usually incarnate human) origin, albeit caused unknowingly; sometimes with other activity also attracted by the force.

Psyche

The nonmaterial part of a psychophysical being.

Rebound

The natural return of a psychic force to its origin, if repelled at its destination; this return can be quite violent.

Relaxation

The loosening of tension, especially a systematic and progressive loosening of tension in the voluntary muscles throughout the body. The creative plan of relaxation is a system in which muscles are first tensed, then

relaxed, the mind meanwhile dwelling on each part of
the body in turn.

Self

An individual's essential identity, referable to one or
other of the main divisions of the total person: (i) higher
self, that part of the psyche that is more elevated than the
rational mind: the higher unconscious, the spirit; (ii)
Lower self, the soul, and the physical body together: the
rational, emotional, instinctual, lower unconscious, and
material levels of the person.

Sensitive (as adjective)

Having acute physical or mental perceptions, or emotional sensibility; (as noun) a person unusually susceptible to psychic influences.

Sephirah (plural, Sephiroth)

One of the ten spheres composing the Qabalistic Tree of
Life. Seven of the Sephiroth represent the modes of
existence characterized by the seven planets of traditional astrology.

Sorcerer, sorceress

An enchanter, usually with inborn and undisciplined
powers.

Splinter personality

A part of the psyche that becomes dissociated from the
rest through severe inhibition (see above), and as a
result functions as a distinct personality or even as a
separate entity.

Subliminal

Literally "below the threshold"; from Liebniz onward, applied to experiences that enter the psyche without coming into consciousness, and can result in overt action still without themselves becoming conscious.

Suggestion

A prompting toward action, speech, or emotion without appeal to the rational mind; a frequent device in psychic attack.

Telepathy

Transference of an idea or of a visualized image directly from mind to mind; now accepted as a fact of experience.

Tree of Life (Qabalistic)

A traditional glyph representing the ten Sephiroth, the "voices from nothing," or modes of being perceptible to humans as existing both in the external universe and in human being's own nature. These are shown as spheres or circles arranged in a particular way that shows their mutual equilibrium.

Unconscious

Those regions of the psyche that lie outside the range of normal human consciousness. The collective unconscious is a repository of the great totality of human inner experience, and notably of the great archetypes (see above); the personal unconscious contains forgotten and repressed material relating to the life of the individual.

Vampire

A being that preys on the life-forces of others; most often used to mean the true vampire, the gross astral or "etheric" body of a deceased person (not, as is popularly supposed, the reanimated corpse) that, having escaped disintegration, proceeds forth from the grave to draw its equally nonmaterial but vital sustenance from its victims, usually while they sleep. The psychic vampire, a living person who, knowingly or not, draws energy from other people to make up for his or her own (usually physical) depletion. The astral vampire, a discarnate being; rarely a whole "earthbound" psyche, sometimes a detached "splinter personality" (see above) and sometimes a debased elemental, preying on human victims.

GET MORE AT **LLEWELLYN.COM**

Visit us online to browse hundreds of our books and decks, plus sign up to receive our e-newsletters and exclusive online offers.

- **Free tarot readings • Spell-a-Day • Moon phases**
- **Recipes, spells, and tips • Blogs • Encyclopedia**
- **Author interviews, articles, and upcoming events**

GET SOCIAL WITH **LLEWELLYN**

Find us on Facebook

www.Facebook.com/LlewellynBooks

Follow us on

twitter

www.Twitter.com/Llewellynbooks

GET BOOKS AT **LLEWELLYN**

LLEWELLYN ORDERING INFORMATION

 Order online: Visit our website at www.llewellyn.com to select your books and place an order on our secure server.

 Order by phone:
- Call toll free within the U.S. at 1-877-NEW-WRLD (1-877-639-9753)
- Call toll free within Canada at 1-866-NEW-WRLD (1-866-639-9753)
- We accept VISA, MasterCard, and American Express

 Order by mail:
Send the full price of your order (MN residents add 6.875% sales tax) in U.S. funds, plus postage and handling to: Llewellyn Worldwide, 2143 Wooddale Drive Woodbury, MN 55125-2989

POSTAGE AND HANDLING
STANDARD (U.S. & Canada):
(Please allow 12 business days)
$25.00 and under, add $4.00.
$25.01 and over, FREE SHIPPING.

INTERNATIONAL ORDERS (airmail only):
$16.00 for one book, plus $3.00 for each additional book.

Visit us online for more shipping options. Prices subject to change.

FREE CATALOG!

To order, call
1-877-
NEW-WRLD
ext. 8236
or visit our
website

Practical Guide to Creative Visualization

Manifest Your Desires

DENNING & PHILLIPS

All things you want must have their start in your mind. The average person uses very little of the full creative power that is potentially his or hers. It's like the power locked in the atom—it's all there, but you have to learn to release it and apply it constructively.

Through an easy series of step-by-step, progressive exercises, your mind is applied to bring desire into realization! Wealth, power, success, happiness, even psychic powers . . . even what we call magickal power and spiritual attainment . . . all can be yours. You can easily develop this completely natural power, and correctly apply it, for your immediate and practical benefit.

0-87542-183-0
264 pp., 5¾₁₆ x 8 $13.99

Practical Guide to Psychic Powers
Awaken Your Sixth Sense

DENNING & PHILLIPS

Because you are missing out on so much without them! Who has not dreamed of possessing powers to move objects without physically touching them, to see at a distance or into the future, to know another's thoughts, to read the past of an object or person, or to find water or mineral wealth by dowsing?

This book is a complete course—teaching you step-by-step how to develop the powers that actually have been yours since birth. Psychic powers are a natural part of your mind; by expanding your mind in this way, you will gain health and vitality, emotional strength, greater success in your daily pursuits, and a new understanding of your inner self.

0-87542-191-1
216 pp., 5³⁄₁₆ x 8, illus. $13.99

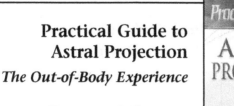

Practical Guide to Astral Projection
The Out-of-Body Experience

DENNING & PHILLIPS

Yes, your consciousness can be sent forth, out of the body, with full awareness, and return with full memory. You can travel through time and space, converse with nonphysical entities, obtain knowledge by nonmaterial means, and experience higher dimensions.

Is there life after death? Are we forever shackled by time and space? The ability to go forth by means of the astral body, or body of light, gives personal assurance of consciousness (and life) beyond the limitations of the physical body. No other answer to these ageless questions is as meaningful as experienced reality.

Guidance is also given to the astral world itself: what to expect, what can be done—including the ecstatic experience of astral sex between two people who project together into this higher world where true union is consummated free of the barriers of physical bodies.

0-87542-181-4
240 pp., 5³⁄₁₆ x 8, photos $13.99

How to Do Psychic Readings Through Touch
TED ANDREWS

What if a chair could speak? What if you could pick up a pen and tell what kind of day its owner had had? What if you could touch someone and know what kind of person he or she truly was—or sense pain or illness? These examples just scratch the surface of the applications of psychometry: the ability to read the psychic imprints that exist upon objects, people, and places.

Everyone is psychic. Unfortunately, most of the time we brush aside our psychic impressions. Now, everyone can learn to develop their own natural sensitivities. *How to Do Psychic Readings Through Touch* will teach you to assess your own abilities and provide you with a step-by-step process for developing your natural psychic abilities, including over twenty-five exercises to heighten your normal sense of touch to new levels of sensitivity.

978-0-7387-0814-0
240 pp., 5³⁄₁₆ x 8, illus. $9.99

Self Hypnosis for a Better Life
WILLIAM W. HEWITT

The sound of your own voice is an incredibly powerful tool for speaking to and reprogramming your subconscious. Now, for the first time, you can select your own self-hypnosis script and record it yourself. *Self-Hypnosis for a Better Life* gives the exact wording for twenty-three unique situations that can be successfully handled with self-hypnosis. Each script is complete in itself and only takes thirty minutes to record. You simply read the script aloud into a tape recorder, then replay the finished tape back to yourself and reap the rewards of self-hypnosis!

Whether you want to eradicate negativity from your life, attract a special romantic partner, solve a problem, be more successful at work, or simply relax, you will find a number of tapes to suit your needs. Become your own hypnotherapist as you design your own self-improvement program, and you can make anything happen.

1-56718-358-1
256 pp., 5³⁄₁₆ x 8, illus.   **$12.99**